SMP 11-16

Book Y4

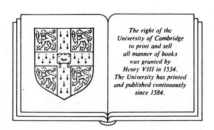

The right of the
University of Cambridge
to print and sell
all manner of books
was granted by
Henry VIII in 1534.
The University has printed
and published continuously
since 1584.

Cambridge University Press

Cambridge
New York   New Rochelle
Melbourne   Sydney

Published by the Press Syndicate of the University of Cambridge
The Pitt Building, Trumpington Street, Cambridge CB2 1RP
32 East 57th Street, New York, NY 10022, USA
10 Stamford Road, Oakleigh, Melbourne 3166, Australia

First published 1987
Reprinted 1987

Illustrations by Chris Evans and David Parkins

Photograph by John Ling

Cover photograph by Graham Portlock
Diagrams and phototypesetting by Parkway Group, London
and Abingdon, and Gecko Limited, Bicester
Printed in Great Britain by Scotprint, Musselburgh, Scotland

British Library cataloguing in publication data
SMP 11–16 yellow series.
  Bk Y4
  1. Mathematics – 1961–
  I. School Mathematics Project
  510   QA39.2
  ISBN 0 521 31478 X

Acknowledgements
The authors and the publisher would like to thank Ordnance Survey
for permission to reproduce the map on page 74 (Crown copyright
reserved).

Contents

1 Selections and arrangements

A Combining choices

A1 This is the lunch menu at a roadside café.

Customers choose one of the three first courses and one of the two second courses.

What different two-course meals can be chosen from the menu?

(Use F to stand for Fish and Chips, and so on.)

Alf's Café

Lunch £1·50

Fish and Chips
or Ham Salad
or Steak pie + chips

Rice pudding
or
Ice cream

A2 This is the lunch menu at a high-class hotel.

What different two-course meals can be chosen from this menu?

Westfield Hotel ★★

Lunch £3·50

Grilled plaice, chipped potatoes
or York ham with salad
or Home cooked steak pie
or Spaghetti bolognaise

Fruit Salad
or Chocolate gateau
or Sherry trifle

A3 This is the dinner menu from the same hotel.

Customers choose a first course, a second course and a third course.

How many different three-course meals can be chosen?

Westfield Hotel ★★

Dinner £6·50

Soup
or Grapefruit

Duck à l'orange & 2 veg.
or Roast groin of beef & 2 veg.
or Grilled trout & 2 veg.

Fruit salad.
or Apple tart
or Banana split

Here again is the menu in question A1.

Fish and Chips
or Ham Salad
or Steak pie + chips

Rice pudding
or
Ice cream

The different two-course meals can be set out in a table, like this.

			2nd course	
			Rice pudding (R)	Ice-cream (I)
1st course	Fish and chips	(F)	FR	FI
	Ham salad	(H)	HR	HI
	Steak pie	(S)	SR	SI

You can see from the table that there are 6 possible meals.
A choice of 3 first courses combined with a choice of 2 sweets gives a choice of 6 two-course meals.

A4 Make a table like the one above for this menu.
Use suitable letters to stand for the items on the menu.

1st course	Rainbow trout or Scampi or Cottage pie or Lamb curry
2nd course	Apple crumble or Banana fritters or Jelly and cream

A5 If there is a choice of 5 first courses and a choice of 4 second courses, how many different two-course meals can be chosen?

Look again at the table at the top of the page. Another way to show the choices is to draw a branching diagram, or **tree diagram**.

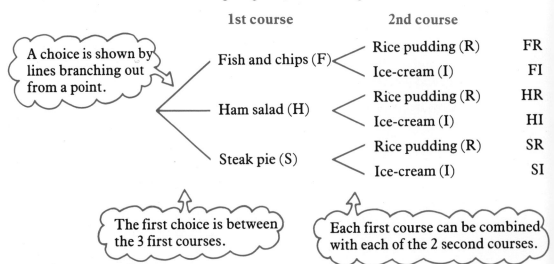

A choice is shown by lines branching out from a point.

1st course	2nd course	
Fish and chips (F)	Rice pudding (R)	FR
	Ice-cream (I)	FI
Ham salad (H)	Rice pudding (R)	HR
	Ice-cream (I)	HI
Steak pie (S)	Rice pudding (R)	SR
	Ice-cream (I)	SI

The first choice is between the 3 first courses.

Each first course can be combined with each of the 2 second courses.

Each route across from left to right represents a two-course meal.

The advantage of the tree diagram is that it can easily be extended to 3 courses or more.

A6 Draw a tree diagram for question A4.

A7 Draw a tree diagram for question A3.

B Non-independent choices

So far, customers have been allowed **a free choice** of first course, a free choice of second course, and so on.
Nobody tells them, for example, that they cannot have ice-cream after fish and chips.

We say that the choice of each course is **independent** of the choice of other courses.

In the next example, the choices are not independent of each other.

Here is the menu.

This time, the customer has a voucher for £1·00, so his meal must not cost more than that.

Also, he is allowed to go without any course, but not allowed to choose more than one item from the same course.

1st course	Soup	20p
	Grapefruit	30p
2nd course	Pork	80p
	Lamb	90p
	Chicken	70p
3rd course	Apple pie	50p
	Ice-cream	30p
	Tapioca	20p

For his first course, he can choose S (soup) or G (grapefruit) or O (nothing).

If he chooses soup, these are his choices for second course. The **total cost so far** is shown.

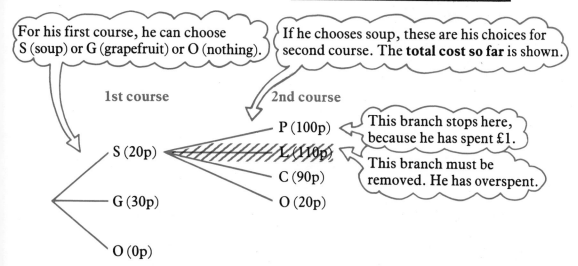

This branch stops here, because he has spent £1.

This branch must be removed. He has overspent.

B1 Copy the diagram and finish it to show all the different meals the customer could have (including nothing at all).

B2 Dawn has £200 to spend on photographic equipment.
She must buy a camera. She could also buy a tripod or a
flashgun or both.

Here are the prices of cameras, tripods and flashguns

Cameras		Tripods		Flashguns	
Pentax	£175	Basic	£25	Low power	£20
Olympus	£150	Super	£35	Medium power	£30
Canon	£210	Pro	£50	High power	£50
Minolta	£180				
Nikon	£220				

Draw a tree diagram showing all the different selections
Dawn could make.

Here is another situation where choices are not independent of each other.

A club has to choose a chairman and a secretary.
There are five people to choose from: A, B, C, D and E.
What different ways are there to fill the two jobs?

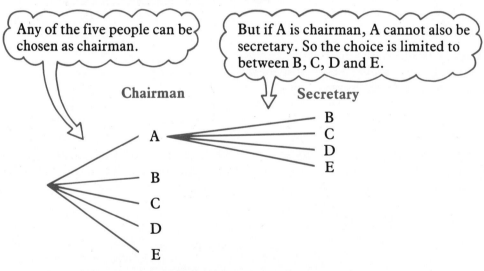

Any of the five people can be chosen as chairman.

But if A is chairman, A cannot also be secretary. So the choice is limited to between B, C, D and E.

B3 (a) Copy the tree diagram and complete it.

(b) How many different ways are there to fill the two jobs?

B4 A sports club has to choose a president and a vice-president.
There are six people to choose from: A, B, C, and D are women
and E and F are men.

The club has a rule that the president and vice-president
cannot both be women or both be men.

Draw a tree diagram to show all the different ways to fill the jobs.

B5 In a competition, entrants have to pick three features of a new car and put them in order of importance: 1st, 2nd, 3rd.

The features they can choose from are

A: Safety belts on all seats   B: Rubber bumpers front and rear
C: Dual braking system   D: Economical engine

(a) Draw a tree diagram to show all the different possible entries. The diagram has three stages of branching: 1st choice, 2nd choice, 3rd choice.

(b) How many different possible entries are there?

(c) Suppose that another feature E is added to the list. How many different possible entries are there now? (Entrants still have to pick three features.)

Permutations

A school Politics Club has invited three MPs to give talks at one of its meetings. They are a Labour MP, a Liberal MP and a Conservative MP.

The club has to decide who is to speak first, who is to speak second and who third.

Here are some of the possible orders of speaking.

    Lab, Lib, Con   Lib, Lab, Con   Con, Lib, Lab   Lab, Con, Lib

Each of these arrangements is called a **permutation** of the three speakers.

A permutation of a group of objects is a way of arranging them in order: 1st, 2nd, 3rd, etc.

Here, for example, are some of the permutations of the four letters A, B, C, D.

    ABCD   ACDB   DCBA   BACD   BDCA

The permutations of a group of objects can be set out in a tree diagram. Here is part of the tree diagram for the three speakers.

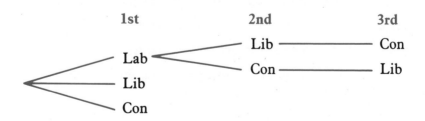

B6 (a) Copy and complete this tree diagram.

(b) How many permutations of the three speakers are there?

5

B7 (a) Draw a tree diagram to show all the permutations of the four letters A, B, C, D. The diagram has four stages of branching: 1st letter, 2nd letter, 3rd letter, 4th letter.

(b) How many permutations of the four letters are there?

C Mixed questions

C1 A camera club holds a photographic competition. Four people, A, B, C and D, enter. There is a 1st prize and a 2nd prize. Each of the four people enters two photos, so it is possible for one person to win both prizes.

Draw a tree diagram to show all the different ways in which the 1st and 2nd prizes could be given to the entrants. (For example, one way is for the 1st prize to go to A and the 2nd to B.)

C2 A tennis team consists of Alice, Brenda and Carol (girls), and David, Edward and Fergus (boys).

One boy and one girl have to be chosen to represent the team at a prizegiving. In how many ways can the pair be chosen?

C3 This diagram shows four railway signals. Each signal shows either **red, single yellow, double yellow** or **green**.

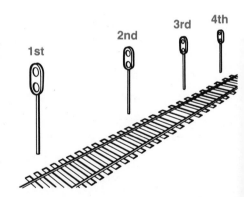

If one signal is green, the next is either green or double yellow.

If one signal is double yellow, the next is single yellow.

If one signal is single yellow, the next is red.

(These are the only restrictions on the colours.)

(a) Draw a tree diagram to show all the possible colour arrangements of the four signals.

(b) How many possible arrangements are there?

D Binary choices

A **binary** choice is a choice between two alternatives, for example yes or no, in or out, head or tail, boy or girl.

This picture shows an indicator in a doctors' waiting room. Each light shows whether a doctor is in or out.

If a doctor's light is on, then he or she is in. If the light is off, then the doctor is out.

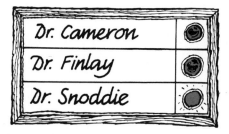

We will assume that the three doctors are in or out independently of each other. We can use a tree diagram to show all the possible ways the three doctors can be in or out.

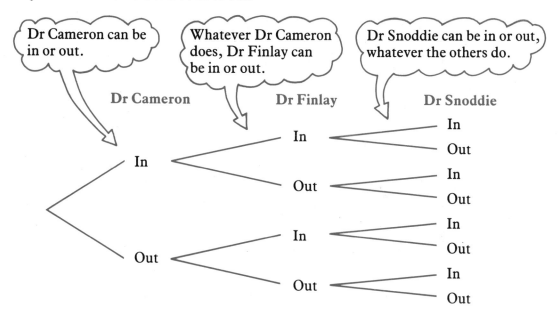

Each choice here is a binary choice, between **in** and **out**.
It is usual to represent the two alternatives in a binary choice by 1 and 0.
We can let 1 mean 'in' and 0 mean 'out'.

The top route across the diagram (In–In–In) can be written 111.
The route In–In–Out is 110, and so on.

D1 Write each of the 8 routes as an arrangement of 1s and 0s.

D2 Suppose a fourth doctor is added to the group. Write out all the possible in–out arrangements using 1 and 0.
How many are there?

If a coin is thrown, it may land **head** or **tail**. This is a binary choice.
We can write 1 for head and 0 for tail.

If three coins are thrown (or the same coin thrown three times) then
the tree diagram showing all possible outcomes is really the same as the
tree diagram for the three doctors on the previous page.

1st coin	2nd coin	3rd coin	Outcome
		1	111
	1	0	110
1		1	101
	0	0	100
		1	011
	1	0	010
0		1	001
	0	0	000

D3 There are 8 possible outcomes when 3 coins are thrown.

(a) How many are there when 4 coins are thrown?

(b) How many are there when 5 coins are thrown?

D4 Explain why the number of outcomes doubles when the
number of coins is increased by 1.

In the examples of the doctors and the coins, the binary choices are
independent of each other.
In the next questions the choices are not independent.

D5 Marimba is governed by four people:
        the President   the First Permanent Secretary
        the Vice-President   the Second Permanent Secretary

To prevent a revolution taking place they keep to strict rules
about who can leave the country.

> If the President leaves the country, then the Vice-President
> must remain, and so must at least one of the Permanent
> Secretaries.
> When the President is in the country, the Vice-President may
> leave but only if both Permanent Secretaries remain.

(a) Draw a tree diagram to show all the allowed combinations
of in and out for the four people.

(b) Use a zero–one code to write down all the combinations that are
allowed. (For example, 1011 means 'President in, Vice-President
out, First Permanent Secretary in, Second Permanent Secretary in'.)

2 Enlargement and volume

A Estimating volumes

A1 (a) How many of the smaller bottles
do you think could be filled
from the larger bottle?

(b) The volume of the smaller bottle
is 0·75 litre. Use your answer
to part (a) to write down an
estimate of the volume of the
larger bottle.

A2 The larger of these two
glasses holds 500 ml
when full.

Estimate the volume
of the smaller glass.
Write down your
estimate.

Keep your answers to
questions A1 and A2.
You will need them
later.

B Enlarging a cube

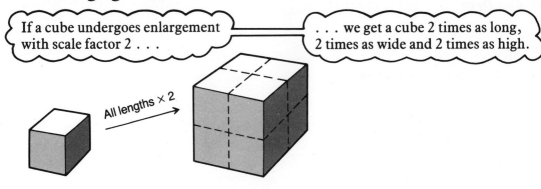

If a cube undergoes enlargement with scale factor 2 . . .

. . . we get a cube 2 times as long, 2 times as wide and 2 times as high.

All lengths × 2

B1 (a) How many times does the volume of the small cube go into the volume of the enlarged cube?

(b) If the small cube's volume is 50 cm³, what is the volume of the enlarged cube?

B2 A cube undergoes enlargement with scale factor 3.

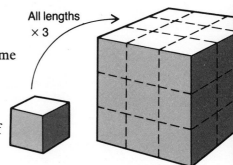

All lengths × 3

(a) How many times does the volume of the small cube go into the volume of the enlarged cube?

(b) If the small cube's volume is 20 cm³, what is the volume of the enlarged cube?

When a cube is enlarged with scale factor 2 its volume is multiplied by **8**.

We say the **volume factor** is 8 when the scale factor is 2.

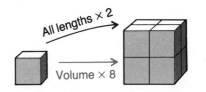

All lengths × 2

Volume × 8

You can think of the volume being multiplied by 2 three times, like this.

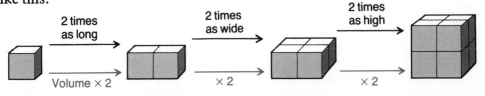

2 times as long

2 times as wide

2 times as high

Volume × 2   × 2   × 2

This explains why the volume is multiplied by 2 × 2 × 2, or 2^3.

B3 A cube is enlarged with a scale factor of 5.

  (a) What is the volume factor of the enlargement?
      (What is the volume multiplied by?)

  (b) The original cube's volume is $10\,cm^3$. What is
      the volume of the enlarged cube?

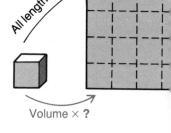

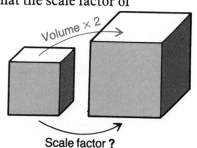

Volume × ?

B4 A cube is enlarged with a scale
       factor of 1·5.

  (a) Calculate the volume factor.

  (b) Calculate the volume of the
      enlarged cube if the volume of
      the original cube is $80\,cm^3$.

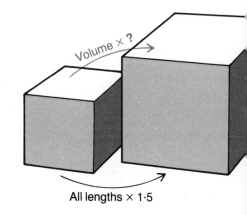

Volume × ?

All lengths × 1·5

B5 Copy and complete this table of scale factors and
       volume factors for enlargements of a cube.

Scale factor	Volume factor
1	1
1·5	
2	8
2·5	

and so on up to 10

B6 **A famous problem from ancient Greece**

A king had an altar of solid gold, in the shape of a cube.
He wanted his goldsmith to make an enlargement of the altar
whose volume would be exactly twice that of the altar itself.

The goldsmith's problem was to decide what the scale factor of
the enlargement should be.

He knew that 1·5 would be too much
because the volume factor would be
3·375.

Use a decimal search to find the scale
factor he needed, to 2 decimal places.

Volume × 2

Scale factor ?

11

C Enlarging other shapes

So far we have been enlarging cubes.
We have found that if the scale factor is 2, the volume factor is 2^3, or 8,
                if the scale factor is 3, the volume factor is 3^3, or 27,
                if the scale factor is 3·5, the volume factor is $3·5^3$, or 42·875,
                and so on.

We can state a general rule.

$$\text{Volume factor} = (\text{Scale factor})^3$$

This rule is true whatever shape you enlarge.

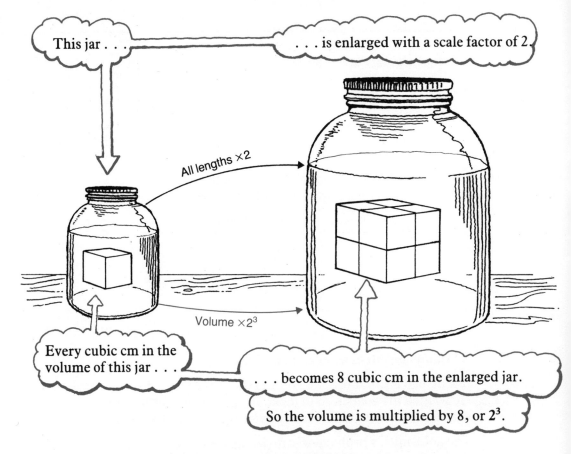

This jar . . .   . . . is enlarged with a scale factor of 2.

All lengths ×2

Volume ×2^3

Every cubic cm in the volume of this jar . . .

. . . becomes 8 cubic cm in the enlarged jar.

So the volume is multiplied by 8, or 2^3.

C1   If the volume of the smaller bottle in the picture above is $12\,\text{cm}^3$, what is the volume of the ×2 enlargement of it?

C2   A glass bottle factory makes two kinds of bottle. The larger kind is an enlargement of the smaller kind with scale factor 3.

     The smaller kind has a volume of $10\,\text{cm}^3$. What is the volume of the larger kind?

C3   Another factory makes two kinds of bottle. The larger kind
       is an enlargement of the smaller kind with scale factor 1·8.

       (a) Calculate the volume factor of the enlargement.

       (b) The smaller kind of bottle has a volume of 60 cm^3.
            Calculate the volume of the larger kind, to the nearest cm^3.

C4   This is a scale drawing of two toothpaste tubes.
       Tube B is an enlargement of tube A.

       (a) Measure the total length of each tube.

       (b) Use the lengths to calculate the scale factor of the enlargement
            from A to B. Write down the scale factor to 2 d.p.

       (c) Calculate the volume factor of the enlargement from A to B.

       (d) The volume of tube A is 40 cm^3. Calculate the volume of
            tube B, to the nearest cm^3.

C5   A factory makes plastic test-tubes for holding liquids. They make
       two types, P and Q. Type Q is an enlargement of type P.

       Type P is 15 cm long and has a volume of 25 cm^3.
       Type Q is 24 cm long.

       (a) Calculate the scale factor of the enlargement from P to Q.

       (b) Calculate the volume factor of the enlargement.

       (c) Calculate the volume of a tube of type Q, to the nearest cm^3.

       (d) The factory makes a third type of tube, R, also an enlargement
            of type P. Type R is 30 cm long. Calculate its volume.

C6 Turn back to the photo of the bottles on page 9.

   (a) Measure the heights in the photo of the two bottles and calculate the scale factor of the enlargement from the smaller bottle to the larger.

   (b) Calculate the volume factor of the enlargement.

   (c) The volume of the smaller bottle is 0·75 litre. Calculate the volume of the larger bottle.

   (d) How good was your estimate of the volume when you first looked at the photo? (See your answer to question A1.) Was your estimate too large or too small?

D Reductions

A reduction can be thought of as an enlargement whose scale factor is less than 1.

The diagram below illustrates a reduction with scale factor 0·6.

Every cubic cm in the larger bottle becomes $0·6 \times 0·6 \times 0·6\,cm^3$ in the smaller bottle.
Once again we get the volume factor by cubing the scale factor.
The volume factor here is $0·6^3 = 0·216$.

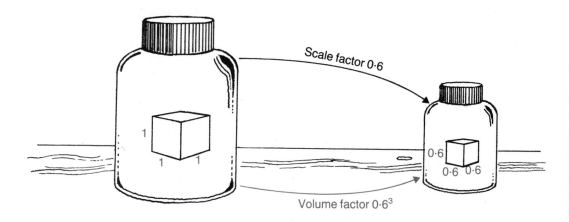

D1 The larger bottle in the picture above has a volume of $9\,cm^3$.

   (a) Calculate the volume of the smaller bottle, to the nearest cm^3.

   (b) Roughly how many small bottles will fill the larger bottle?

D2 A and B are two bottles. B is a reduction of A with scale factor 0·7.

   (a) Calculate the volume factor of the reduction.

   (b) Calculate the volume of B if that of A is $400\,cm^3$.

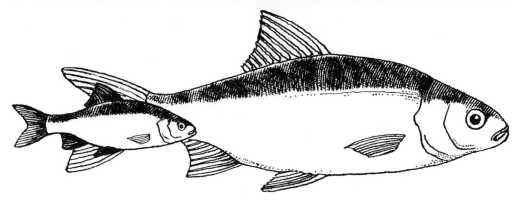

D3 The young fish in this picture is approximately a ×0·4 reduction of the adult fish.

(a) Calculate the volume factor of the reduction.

(b) If the adult fish weighs 800 g, how much would you expect the young fish to weigh?

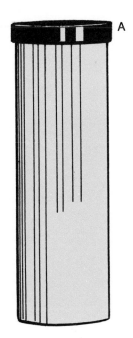

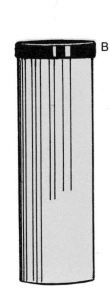

D4 This is a scale drawing of two containers. Container B is a reduction of container A.

(a) Measure the height of each container in the drawing.

(b) From the height calculate the scale factor of the reduction from A to B, to 2 d.p.

(c) Calculate the volume factor of the reduction.

(d) Container A has a volume of 500 ml. Calculate the volume of container B.

D5 An ordinary tea-cup is 5·5 cm tall and holds 120 ml.
The tea-cups in a child's tea-set are reductions of ordinary tea-cups. They are 2·5 cm tall.

(a) Calculate the scale factor of the reduction from an ordinary cup to a child's cup.

(b) Calculate the volume factor of the reduction.

(c) Calculate the volume of the child's cup.

D6 Turn back to the picture of the two glasses on page 9.

    (a) Measure the height of each glass in the picture.

    (b) From your measurements calculate the scale factor of the reduction from the larger glass to the smaller.

    (c) Calculate the volume factor of the reduction.

    (d) The larger glass holds 500 ml. Calculate the volume of the smaller glass.

    (e) Compare the volume with your estimate (question A2). Did you overestimate the volume or underestimate it?

E Effects of enlargement on length, area and volume

If an object is enlarged with scale factor k,

    lengths are multiplied by k,

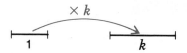

    areas are multiplied by k^2,

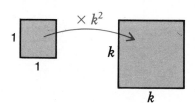

    volumes are multiplied by k^3.

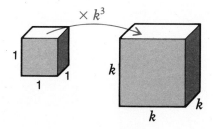

E1 A firm of vehicle manufacturers designs a new road tanker.
They show a model of the new tanker at an exhibition.
The model is made to a scale of $\frac{1}{10}$ full size, so the real tanker is an enlargement of the model with scale factor 10.

    (a) The model tanker will hold 75 litres of liquid. How much will the real tanker hold?

    (b) The inside surface of the tank has to be coated with copper.
The area of the inside surface in the model is $1 \cdot 1 \, \text{m}^2$.
What is the area of the inside surface in the real tanker?

E2 The photo above shows a scale model of an old coastal barge. The scale of the model is $\frac{1}{60}$ full size.

Here are some sentences describing the model barge and the real barge. Write down the measurements which go in the blanks.

(a) 1 cm in the model represents . . . cm, or . . . m, in the real barge.

(b) A square 1 cm by 1 cm in the model represents a square . . . cm by . . . cm, or . . . m by . . . m, in the real barge.

(c) So 1 cm^2 in the model represents . . . m^2 in the real barge.

(d) A cube 1 cm by 1 cm by 1 cm in the model represents a cube . . . cm by . . . cm by . . . cm, or . . . m by . . . m by . . . m, in the real barge.

(e) So 1 cm^3 in the model represents . . . m^3 on the real barge.

(f) Here is some information about the model barge. Make a similar table of information about the real barge.

Length of hull	29 cm
Maximum width of hull	10·5 cm
Volume of hold	380 cm^3
Area of sail[1]	3500 cm^2
Length of anchor chain	13 cm
Length of ladder	8·5 cm
Number of rungs on ladder	13
Total area of deck	240 cm^2
Percentage of total volume below water, when fully laden	85%
Angle at bow	130°
Speed	4 cm/s

[1] Sail not shown in photo

17

E3 The drawing below shows a model of a gas-filled balloon, made of fabric. The table gives some information about the model.

Length	1·5 m
Volume	0·28 m³
Area of fabric	3·3 m²

The upward force on the balloon is 9·1 newtons for each cubic metre of gas in it.

The downward force is 1·6 newtons for each square metre of fabric.

The balloon will fly provided the upward force is greater than the downward force.

(a) Calculate the upward force on the model balloon.

(b) Calculate the downward force on the model balloon.

(c) Will the model balloon fly?

Another balloon is made of the same fabric. It is an enlargement of the model and is 2·4 m long.

(d) Calculate the scale factor of the enlargement.

(e) Calculate the volume of the enlarged balloon.

(f) Calculate the area of its fabric.

(g) The upward and downward forces are related to the volume and area in the same way as before. Find out if the enlarged balloon will fly.

(h) Suppose the original model is enlarged with scale factor k. Write down expressions for
  (i) the volume of the enlarged balloon
  (ii) the area of the fabric of the enlarged balloon
  (iii) the upward force on the enlarged balloon
  (iv) the downward force on the enlarged balloon.

(i) Calculate the upward and downward forces for different values of k, as shown in the table below. Copy the table and fill it in.

Scale factor k	1·6	1·8	2·0	2·2	2·4	2·6
Upward force, in newtons						
Downward force, in newtons						

(Continued on next page.)

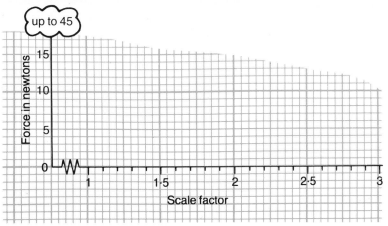

(j) Draw axes, using the scales shown here.
Using the same pair of axes, draw two graphs, one showing the upward force and one the downward force. Label each graph clearly.

(k) For what value of k will the balloon just be able to fly?

Effects of size in animals

These extracts come from an article by the biologist J. B. S. Haldane (1892–1964).

Consider a giant man sixty feet high – about the height of Giant Pope and Giant Pagan in the illustrated *Pilgrim's Progress* of my childhood. These monsters were not only ten times as high as Christian, but ten times as wide and ten times as thick, so their total weight was a thousand times his, or about eighty to ninety tons. Unfortunately the cross-sections of their bones were only a hundred times those of Christian, so that every square inch of giant bone had to support ten times the weight borne by a square inch of human bone. As the human thigh-bone breaks under about ten times the human weight, Pope and Pagan would have broken their thighs every time they took a step. This was doubtless why they were sitting down in the picture I remember. But it lessens one's respect for Christian and Jack the Giant Killer.

Gravity, a mere nuisance to Christian, was a terror to Pope and Pagan. To the mouse and any smaller animal it presents practically no dangers. You can drop a mouse down a three thousand-foot mine shaft, and, on arriving at the bottom, it gets a slight shock and walks away. A rat would probably be killed, though it can fall safely from the eleventh floor of a building; a man is killed, a horse splashes. For the resistance presented to movement by the air is proportional to the surface of the moving object. Divide an animal's length, breadth and height each by ten; its weight is reduced to a thousandth, but its surface only to a hundredth. So the resistance to falling in the case of the small animal is relatively ten times greater than the driving force.

3 Linear equations

A Intersecting lines

The equation $3x + 2y = 12$ is called a **linear equation** because its graph is a straight line.

The easiest way to draw the graph is to find where it crosses the axes.

When x is 0, then $3 \times 0 + 2y = 12$ $2y = 12$ $y = 6$ So the graph goes through $(0, 6)$.	When y is 0, then $3x + 2 \times 0 = 12$ $3x = 12$ $x = 4$ So the graph goes through $(4, 0)$.	So the graph looks like this. 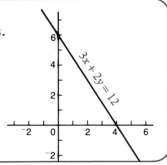

A1 (a) Draw the graph of $3x + 2y = 12$.

(b) On the same axes, draw the graph of $x + y = 5$.

(c) Write down the coordinates of the point of intersection of the two lines.

The coordinates of the point of intersection can be calculated without drawing the graphs.

We know that the first line consists of all the points whose coordinates fit (or **satisfy**) the equation $3x + 2y = 12$.
Similarly the second line consists of all the points whose coordinates satisfy the equation $x + y = 5$.

The coordinates of the point of intersection must satisfy both equations.

So we need to find the **common solution** of the equations

(1) $3x + 2y = 12$
(2) $x + y = 5$

We can eliminate x by multiplying equation (2) by 3.

$3x + 3y = 15$

Now we subtract equation (1) from the new equation.

$(3x + 3y) - (3x + 2y) = 15 - 1$
$3x + 3y - 3x - 2y = 3$
$y = 3$

Now we know that y is 3, we can find x by using equation (2).

$x + 3 = 5$
$x = 2$

So the point of intersection is $(2, 3)$.

20

A2 Find the coordinates of the point of intersection of the lines
$6x + y = 6$ and $2x + 3y = 10$.

A3 (a) Draw axes with x and y from $^-10$ to 10.

Draw the graphs of $x + 2y = 10$ and $2x + 3y = 13$ on the same axes.

From your diagram find the coordinates of the point of intersection of the two lines.

(b) Now calculate the coordinates of the point of intersection by finding the common solution of the two equations.

A4 Find the point of intersection of each of these pairs of lines.

(a) $4x + y = 17$ (b) $2x - y = 1$ (c) $3x - y = 1$
$x + 3y = 7$ $x + y = 8$ $2x + 4y = 17$

A5 At what point will these lines meet if extended?

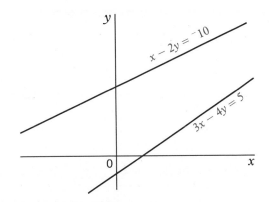

A6 The three lines

$$x + 5y = 53$$
$$2x + y = 25$$
$$4x + 5y = 107$$

make a triangle.

Find the coordinates of the corners of the triangle.

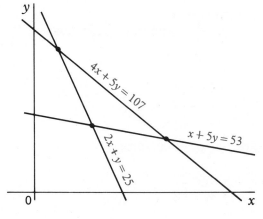

A7 Find out whether the three lines $x + y = 13$, $15x - 23y = 5$ and $3x - y = 19$ all have a common point.

A8 The three lines $x + y = 5$, $3x - 4y = 22$ and $2x + 5y = k$ do have a common point.

What is the value of k?

B Multiplying both equations

Suppose we want to solve the equations

(1) $\quad 3x + 4y = 26$
(2) $\quad 5x + 6y = 40$

It looks as though we can't find a number to multiply one of the equations by.
We can't easily eliminate x, because $5x$ is not a multiple of $3x$, and we can't easily eliminate y, because $6y$ is not a multiple of $4y$.

But if we multiply equation (1) by 5 and equation (2) by 3, we get $15x$ in both equations.

Multiply equation (1) by 5.

$$5(3x + 4y) = 5 \times 26$$
$$15x + 20y = 130$$

Multiply equation (2) by 3.

$$3(5x + 6y) = 3 \times 40$$
$$15x + 18y = 120$$

Now we can subtract.

$$(15x + 20y) - (15x + 18y) = 130 - 120$$
$$15x + 20y - 15x - 18y = 10$$
$$2y = 10$$
$$y = 5$$

Putting y equal to 5 in equation (1), we get

$$3x + 20 = 26$$
$$3x = 6$$
$$x = 2$$

We can check that $x = 2$, $y = 5$ fits equation (2). $\quad 5 \times 2 + 6 \times 5 = 40 \checkmark$

B1 (a) In the working above, we eliminated x.
How could you eliminate y from the same pair of equations?

(b) Solve the equations by eliminating y.

B2 (a) Solve the equations $\quad$ (1) $2x + 3y = 13$
(2) $3x + 4y = 16$
by eliminating x.

(b) Solve the same pair of equations by eliminating y.

B3 Solve the equations $\quad$ (1) $5x + 6y = 28$
(2) $7x + 8y = 40$

B4 Solve the equations $\quad$ (1) $8x + 3y = 12$
(2) $5x - 4y = 31$

B5 Solve the equations $\quad$ (1) $4x - 3y = 14$
(2) $5x - 2y = 21$

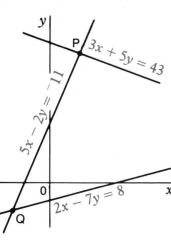

B6 (a) Find the coordinates of P in the diagram on the left.

(b) Find the coordinates of Q.

(c) Where do the lines $3x + 5y = 43$ and $2x - 7y = 8$ intersect?

B7 Find all the points of intersection of the three lines

$$3x + 5y = 24 \qquad 2x - y = 3 \qquad 6x + 10y = 22$$

C Special cases

You may have found something unexpected in question B7.
We shall now look at this in more detail, but with a different example.

Suppose we want to find the point of intersection of the lines
(1) $8x + 12y = 60$
(2) $2x + 3y = 12$

We could start by eliminating x.
To do this, we multiply equation (2) by 4.

$$4(2x + 3y) = 4 \times 12$$
$$8x + 12y = 48$$

When we subtract equation (1), we get

$$(8x + 12y) - (8x + 12y) = 60 - 48$$
$$0 = 12$$

We end up with a statement '$0 = 12$' which cannot possibly be true!
There is something peculiar about the two equations we started with.
When we draw their graphs, we see what it is.

The two lines $8x + 12y = 60$ and $2x + 3y = 12$
are **parallel** to each other. They have **no** point
of intersection.

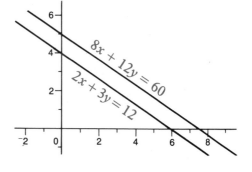

Equation (1) says that $8x + 12y$ has to be 60.
Equation (2) says that $2x + 3y$ is 12, so $8x + 12y$
has to be 48.

But $8x + 12y$ cannot be both 60 and 48.

We say equations (1) and (2) are **inconsistent**.
They contradict each other.

C1 (a) Draw the graphs of the lines $3x - 5y = 15$ and $9x - 15y = 90$.

(b) Try to solve the pair of equations. Are they consistent?

C2 What happens when you try to solve $2x + 3y = 12$ and $6x + 9y = 36$?
Are the equations consistent? Draw their graphs.

This is what you get when you try to solve $2x + 3y = 12$ and $6x + 9y = 36$.

$$(1) \quad 2x + 3y = 12$$
$$(2) \quad 6x + 9y = 36$$

Eliminate x. Multiply equation (1) by 3. $\qquad\qquad 6x + 9y = 36$

Subtract the new equation from equation (2). $\qquad\qquad 0 = 0$

We end up with a statement which is true, but which does not help us to solve the equations.

The reason is that equation (2) is not really a different equation from equation (1). The information in equation (2) is already contained in (1), because if $2x + 3y$ is 12 then $6x + 9y$ must be 36.

The graph of equation (2) is exactly the same line as the graph of equation (1).

We say that equations (1) and (2) have **infinitely many solutions**, because **every** point on the one graph fits both equations.

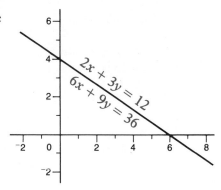

C3 Try to solve each of these pairs of equations.
If they have one solution, write it in the form $x = \ldots, y = \ldots$
If they are inconsistent, write 'no solution'.
If the second equation contains no more information than the first, write 'infinitely many solutions'.

(a) $3x + 2y = 18$
$\quad\;\, 6x + 4y = 36$

(b) $4x + 5y = 40$
$\quad\;\, 12x + 15y = 100$

(c) $3x + 4y = 24$
$\quad\;\, x + 2y = 12$

(d) $\quad 3x - 2y = 7$
$\quad\;\, {}^-6x + 4y = 3$

(e) $\;{}^-4x + 8y = 16$
$\quad\;\, x - 2y = {}^-8$

(f) $4x - \; y = 16$
$\quad\;\, 3x - 2y = 7$

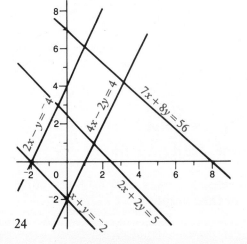

C4 The diagram on the left shows the graphs of five equations. Decide whether each of these pairs of equations has no solution, one solution, or infinitely many solutions.

(a) $2x - y \; = {}^-4, \quad 7x + 8y = 56$

(b) $\quad x + y \; = {}^-2, \quad 7x + 8y = 56$

(c) $2x - y \; = {}^-4, \quad 4x - 2y = 4$

(d) $2x + 2y = 5, \qquad x + y \; = {}^-2$

(e) $2x + 2y = 5, \quad 7x + 8y = 56$

24

4 Angle relationships

A Review of angle relationships

An angle of 180° is just a straight line.

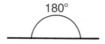

So angles on a straight line must add up to 180°.

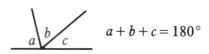

$a + b + c = 180°$

A1 Calculate the lettered angles.

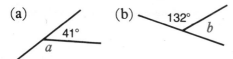

(a) 41° a

(b) 132° b

(c) 28° c 51°

When two straight lines cross, they make four angles. The angles which are opposite each other are called **vertically opposite** angles.

Angles a and c are vertically opposite.
Angles b and d are vertically opposite.

Vertically opposite angles are equal.

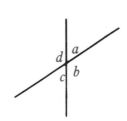

A2 Calculate the lettered angles.

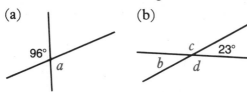

(a) 96° a

(b) c 23° b d

(c) f g e h 77° 38°

In this diagram, a set of parallel lines is crossed by another line. (Parallel lines are shown by arrows.) The angles marked in red are called **corresponding** angles.

Corresponding angles are equal.

Here is the same diagram with a different set of corresponding angles marked.

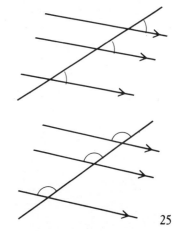

A3 Calculate the angles marked with letters.

(a)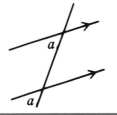

(b)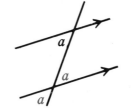

(c)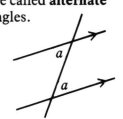

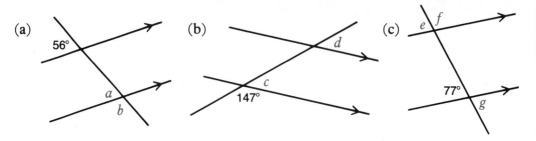

The angles marked *a* are corresponding angles. So they must be equal.

The angles marked in red are vertically opposite. So they must be equal.

So the two angles marked here must be equal. They are called **alternate** angles.

You can think of alternate angles as the angles of a Z. Alternate angles are equal.

A4 Calculate the angles marked with letters.

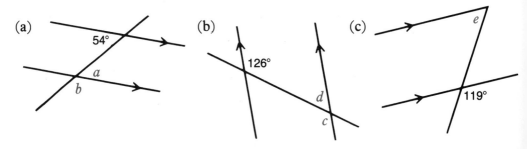

(a)

(b)

(c)

The angles of a triangle add up to 180°.

A5 Calculate the lettered angles.

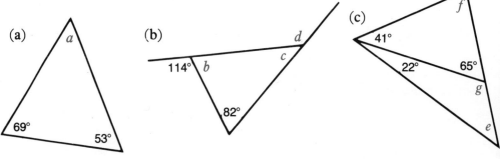

(a)

(b)

(c)

26

B Deduction

Joe Soap is in court, charged with committing a bank robbery.
His lawyer is trying to prove that Joe Soap could not have done it.

She points out that these four statements are all true:

(1) The bank is in London.
(2) It was robbed at 2:30 p.m.
(3) Joe Soap was in Glasgow at 2:15 p.m. that day.
(4) It is impossible to get from Glasgow to London in 15 minutes.

From these four statements the lawyer **deduces** that another statement
must be true:

Joe Soap could not have carried out the robbery.

Similarly, in mathematics we can **deduce** statements from others
which we know to be true.

Starting from these two statements:

(1) Angles on a straight line add up to 180°,
(2) Alternate angles are equal,

it is possible to deduce that the angles of a triangle must add up to 180°.
Question B1 shows how.

B1 The diagram shows a triangle ABC.
The extra line through A is parallel to BC.

(a) Draw the diagram. Mark another
angle which must be equal to p.
Give the reason why it is equal
to p.

(b) Mark another angle which must be
equal to q. Give the reason why.

(c) Why must the angles p, r and q
add up to 180°?

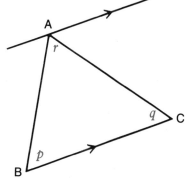

From the fact that the angles of a triangle add up to 180°, we can
deduce that the angles of a quadrilateral must add up to 360°.
Question B2 shows how.

B2 The diagram shows a quadrilateral ABCD
with one diagonal drawn.

(a) Write down each angle of the quadrilateral
in terms of the letters u, v, w, x, y and z.

(b) Explain why the four angles of the
quadrilateral must add up to 360°.

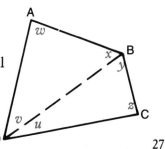

27

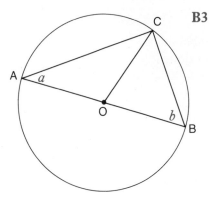

B3 The angle in a semicircle

In this diagram AB is the diameter of a circle.
O is the centre of the circle. C is a point on the circle.

Draw the diagram.

(a) Explain why triangle AOC is an isosceles triangle.

(b) On your diagram mark another angle equal to a.

(c) Mark another angle equal to b, and explain why it must be equal to b.

(d) Write down an expression, in terms of a and b, for
   (i) the angle ACB
   (ii) the sum of the three angles of triangle ABC

(e) Use what you know about the sum of the angles of a triangle to explain why angle ACB is a right-angle.

The fact you have just proved in question B3 is usually stated:

The angle in a semicircle is a right-angle.

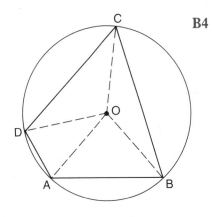

B4 ABCD is a quadrilateral whose four vertices are on a circle. (It is called a 'cyclic' quadrilateral.) O is the centre of the circle.

Draw the diagram.

(a) Explain why each of the triangles OAB, OBC, OCD and ODA is isosceles.

(b) On your diagram mark one pair of equal angles p, another pair q, another pair r and another pair s.

(c) Using what you know about the sum of the angles of a quadrilateral, explain why
   (i) angle ABC + angle ADC = 180°
   (ii) angle BCD + angle BAD = 180°

*B5 In the diagram for question B4, the centre of the circle is inside the quadrilateral.

Prove that the results are still true when the centre is outside the quadrilateral.

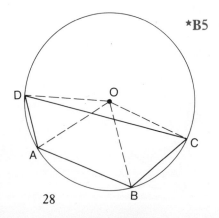

28

C Interior angles of a polygon

Any shape with straight sides is called a **polygon**.

Each corner of a polygon is called a **vertex**.

The angles at the corners are called the **interior angles** of the polygon.

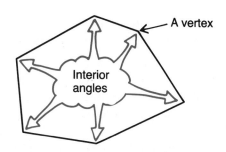

A vertex

Interior angles

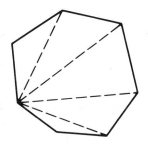

C1 A polygon can be split into triangles by drawing the diagonals from one vertex.

How many triangles do you get if you draw the diagonals from one vertex of

(a) a 6-sided polygon   (b) a 9-sided polygon

(c) a 20-sided polygon   (d) an n-sided polygon

C2 Use this diagram to explain why the interior angles of a 5-sided polygon must add up to 540°.

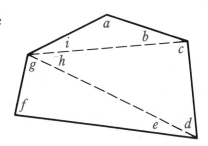

C3 What is the total of all the interior angles of

(a) a 6-sided polygon   (b) a 9-sided polygon   (c) an n-sided polygon

In a **regular** polygon, all the sides are of equal length and all the interior angles are equal.

C4 In question C2, you showed that the total of all the interior angles of a 5-sided polygon must be 540°.

If the 5-sided polygon is regular, what must the size of each angle be?

C5 Use your answers to question C3 to find the size of each interior angle of

(a) a regular 6-sided polygon   (b) a regular 9-sided polygon
(c) a regular n-sided polygon

29

D Exterior angles of a polygon

A robot which can move about on a flat surface is
programmed to obey these instructions:

> Start pointing north.
> Move forward 100 metres, then turn 30° clockwise.
> Move forward another 100 metres, then turn 30°
> clockwise, and so on.

The diagram below shows the path of the robot.

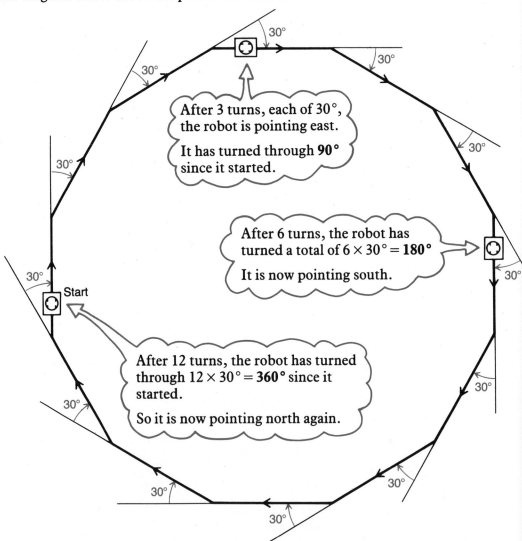

After 3 turns, each of 30°,
the robot is pointing east.

It has turned through **90°**
since it started.

After 6 turns, the robot has
turned a total of $6 \times 30° = $ **180°**

It is now pointing south.

After 12 turns, the robot has turned
through $12 \times 30° = $ **360°** since it
started.

So it is now pointing north again.

The path of the robot is a regular 12-sided polygon.
In the diagram each side has been extended in one direction as you
go round the polygon.

Each of the angles of 30° is called an **exterior angle** of the polygon.

D1 This diagram shows a regular 10-sided polygon. Each exterior angle is marked *e*.

Think of a robot going round the polygon. After turning 10 times, it will be pointing in the same direction as it was to start with.

What must the size of *e* be?

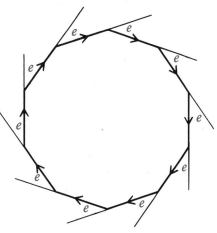

D2 Calculate the size of each exterior angle of a regular polygon with

(a) 8 sides   (b) 15 sides   (c) 20 sides   (d) 40 sides   (e) *n* sides

D3 When you know the size of each exterior angle of a regular polygon, you can calculate the size of each interior angle.

This diagram shows a part of the regular 12-sided polygon on the opposite page.

Calculate the size of the interior angle *i*.

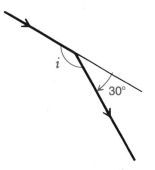

D4 Calculate the size of each interior angle of the regular polygon in question D1.

D5 Use the answers to question D2 to calculate the interior angle of each regular polygon.

D6 Calculate the interior angle of a regular polygon with

(a) 100 sides   (b) 1000 sides   (c) 10 000 sides   (d) 100 000 sides

What happens as the number of sides gets larger and larger?

D7 The exterior angles of a regular polygon are each 20°. How many sides must the polygon have?

D8 How many sides does a regular polygon have if each interior angle is

(a) 160°   (b) 165°   (c) 170°   (d) 175°   (e) 179°

D9 The course for a sailing race is clockwise round a square ABCD.

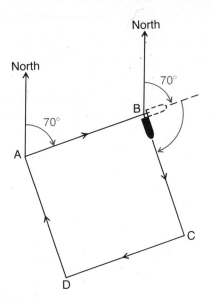

The first 'leg' of the race is on a bearing of 070° (70° measured clockwise from north).

(a) What angle does a boat turn through when it gets to B?

(b) What is the bearing of the second leg of the race, B to C?

(c) Calculate the bearing of the third leg, C to D.

(d) Calculate the bearing of the fourth leg, D to A.

D10 The course for another race is clockwise round an equilateral triangle PQR. The bearing of the first leg, P to Q, is 110°. Calculate the bearings of each of the other legs.

Angles on a polyhedron: an investigation

A **polyhedron** is a solid with flat faces.

This polyhedron has four triangular faces and one quadrilateral face.

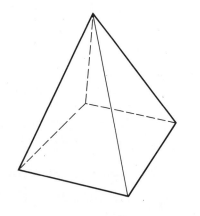

The sum of the angles of each triangle is 180°.

The sum of the angles of each quadrilateral is 360°.

So the total of all the angles of all the faces is $(4 \times 180°) + 360° = 1080°$.

Investigate the relationship between the total of all the angles of all the faces of a polyhedron and the number of vertices of the polyhedron.

5 Algebraic fractions

A Multiplication

If we write '$\frac{2}{3}$' we can mean '$2 \div 3$' or we can mean 'two-thirds'.

But '$2 \div 3$' is equivalent to two-thirds. You can see why if you think about it like this:

Imagine that you have 2 identical cakes, to be shared equally by 3 girls. So you are dividing 2 by 3.	If you have only 1 cake, each girl would get $\frac{1}{3}$ of a cake.	But as you have 2 cakes, each girl will get 2 times as much, or $\frac{2}{3}$. So $2 \div 3 = \frac{2}{3}$.

So it does not matter whether we think of $\frac{2}{3}$ as a division or as a fraction.

An **algebraic fraction** is any expression of the form $\dfrac{\text{something}}{\text{something else}}$.

For example, these are all algebraic fractions: $\dfrac{a}{b}, \dfrac{a}{3}, \dfrac{ax^2}{bx}, \dfrac{3p}{p+q}$.

The rules for dealing with algebraic fractions come from the rules for ordinary fractions. In this section we look at multiplication.

Multiplying a fraction by a whole number

Suppose a dentist has 5 appointments, each lasting $\frac{3}{4}$ hour.

The total length of the appointments is $\frac{3}{4} \times 5$ or $5 \times \frac{3}{4}$ hours. This comes to $\frac{15}{4}$ hours (which is actually $3\frac{3}{4}$ hours, but this does not matter here).
Notice that $\frac{3}{4} \times 5 = \frac{3 \times 5}{4}$.

This rule applies to algebraic fractions as well. For example,

$$\frac{a}{b} \times c = \frac{ac}{b} \qquad x \times \frac{3y}{z} = \frac{3xy}{z} \qquad s \times \frac{t+u}{v} = \frac{s(t+u)}{v}$$

> **A1** Write each of these as a single algebraic fraction.
>
> (a) $u \times \dfrac{v}{w}$ (b) $\dfrac{2r}{s} \times t$ (c) $\dfrac{x}{y} \times 4$ (d) $\dfrac{a+b}{c} \times d$

A2 Write each of these as a single algebraic fraction.

(a) $a \times \dfrac{1}{b}$ (b) $x \times \dfrac{a+b}{2c}$ (c) $\dfrac{f}{g} \times (r+s)$ (d) $y \times \dfrac{5}{m+n}$

When you multiply $\dfrac{3}{4}$ by $\dfrac{5}{8}$, the result is $\dfrac{3 \times 5}{4 \times 8}$, or $\dfrac{15}{32}$.

Similarly, when you multiply $\dfrac{a}{b}$ by $\dfrac{c}{d}$, the result is $\dfrac{a \times c}{b \times d}$, or $\dfrac{ac}{bd}$.

Multiplication is the easiest operation with fractions, but sometimes you have to remember to write **brackets**. For example, $\dfrac{a}{b} \times \dfrac{c+d}{e} = \dfrac{a(c+d)}{be}$

A3 Write each of these as a single algebraic fraction.

(a) $\dfrac{p}{q} \times \dfrac{r}{s}$ (b) $\dfrac{2}{r} \times \dfrac{s}{t}$ (c) $\dfrac{a}{b} \times \dfrac{c}{d-e}$ (d) $\dfrac{2}{r} \times \dfrac{5}{s}$ (e) $\dfrac{a+b}{c} \times$

A4 Write each of these as a single fraction.

(a) $\dfrac{3}{x} \times \dfrac{y}{5}$ (b) $\dfrac{x-y}{4} \times \dfrac{3}{r+s}$ (c) $\dfrac{x}{a} \times \dfrac{x}{b}$ (d) $\dfrac{u}{3a} \times \dfrac{v}{2a}$

The whole number 5 can also be thought of as the 'fraction' $\dfrac{5}{1}$.
Multiplying a fraction by a whole number is then a special case of multiplying by a fraction.

For example, $\dfrac{3}{8} \times 5 = \dfrac{3}{8} \times \dfrac{5}{1} = \dfrac{15}{8}$

Similarly, $\dfrac{a}{b} \times c = \dfrac{a}{b} \times \dfrac{c}{1} = \dfrac{ac}{b}$

A5 Write each of these as a single fraction.

(a) $\dfrac{2p}{q} \times rs$ (b) $b \times \dfrac{c+d}{e+f}$ (c) $(p+q) \times \dfrac{r}{s}$

(d) $\dfrac{3}{j-k} \times (g-h)$ (e) $\dfrac{3}{4} \times (a+b)$ (f) $\dfrac{x}{y} \times 3x$

A6 Just as a^2 means $a \times a$, so $\left(\dfrac{a}{b}\right)^2$ means $\dfrac{a}{b} \times \dfrac{a}{b} = \dfrac{a^2}{b^2}$.

Write these without brackets.

(a) $\left(\dfrac{a}{3}\right)^2$ (b) $\left(\dfrac{5}{p}\right)^2$ (c) $\left(\dfrac{pq}{r}\right)^2$ (d) $\left(\dfrac{f}{2}\right)^2 \times \left(\dfrac{5}{h}\right)^2$ (e) $\dfrac{a}{2} \times \left(\dfrac{b}{3}\right)^2$

B Simplifying fractions

The fraction $\frac{15}{20}$ can be simplified to $\frac{3}{4}$. You do this by

dividing 'top and bottom' by 5, because 5 is a factor of both 15 and 20.

Another way to look at it is this: $\frac{15}{20} = \frac{3 \times 5}{4 \times 5} = \frac{3}{4} \times \frac{5}{5}$

'5 fifths' is 1.

$$= \frac{3}{4} \times 1$$

$$= \frac{3}{4}$$

The number 5 appears as a factor of the top (15) and of the bottom (20).

It is 'cancelled out' because multiplying by $\frac{5}{5}$ has no effect.

The same idea is used to simplify algebraic fractions. For example,

$$\frac{ac}{bc} = \frac{a \times c}{b \times c} = \frac{a}{b} \times \frac{c}{c} = \frac{a}{b} \times 1 = \frac{a}{b}.$$

Usually we miss out the middle steps and think it out like this:

$$\frac{ac}{bc} = \frac{a\cancel{c}}{b\cancel{c}} = \frac{a}{b}.$$

B1 Simplify these.

(a) $\frac{pq}{pr}$ (b) $\frac{3x}{5x}$ (c) $\frac{2ab}{3a}$ (d) $\frac{fgh}{fhj}$ (e) $\frac{6uv}{7vw}$ (f) $\frac{x}{7x}$

B2 Simplify $\frac{ax^2}{bx}$. (Remember that x^2 means xx.)

B3 Simplify these.

(a) $\frac{2a^2}{a}$ (b) $\frac{ab}{a^2c}$ (c) $\frac{3pq^2}{5q}$ (d) $\frac{7mbc}{10m^2a}$ (e) $\frac{4x^2y}{3ax^2}$

B4 The circle in this diagram touches the sides of the square. The radius of the circle is r.

(a) What is the length of each side of the square, in terms of r?
(b) Write an expression for the area of the square, in terms of r.
(c) Write an expression for the ratio $\frac{\text{Area of circle}}{\text{Area of square}}$, and simplify it.

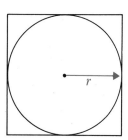

The fraction $\dfrac{a^2bc}{acd}$ can be simplified by cancelling the factors

a and c of the top and bottom: $\dfrac{a^2bc}{acd} \left(= \dfrac{\cancel{a}ab\cancel{c}}{\cancel{a}\cancel{c}d}\right) = \dfrac{ab}{d}$.

Sometimes numbers can be cancelled as well.

For example, $\dfrac{6abc^2}{8b^2c} \left(= \dfrac{\cancel{6}^3}{\cancel{8}4} \times \dfrac{ab\cancel{c}c}{\cancel{b}bc}\right) = \dfrac{3ac}{4b}$.

B5 Simplify these.

(a) $\dfrac{12pq^2r}{3pqr^2}$ (b) $\dfrac{10ab^2c}{15a^2bc^2}$ (c) $\dfrac{7x^2y^2z}{4xz^2}$ (d) $\dfrac{4u^2}{3v} \times \dfrac{6v^2}{2u}$

B6 A is the area of a circle of radius r, so $A = \pi r^2$.
C is the circumference of the circle, so $C = 2\pi r$.

(a) Write down an expression for C^2 in terms of π and r, without brackets.

(b) Show that the ratio $\dfrac{C^2}{A}$ is equal to 4π.

'Cancelling' can only be done when the cancelled letter or number is **a factor** of the top and the bottom of the fraction.

For example, it is not possible to cancel the 3's in $\dfrac{3 + 4}{3 \times 5}$.

If you 'cancel' the 3's you would get $\dfrac{\overset{1}{\cancel{3}} + 4}{\underset{1}{\cancel{3}} \times 5} = \dfrac{5}{5} = 1$, but $\dfrac{3 + 4}{3 \times 5} = \dfrac{7}{15}$, not 1.

This 'cancelling' is wrong because 3 is **not a factor** of $3 + 4$.

In the fraction $\dfrac{a + b}{ac}$, a is **not** a factor of the top expression $a + b$, because the expression is a **plus** something, not a **times** something. So the a's **cannot** be cancelled in the fraction $\dfrac{a + b}{ac}$.

In the fraction $\dfrac{ax + b}{ac}$, a is **not** a factor of the top expression; it is a factor of only part of it (ax), not the whole of it. So here again, the a's **cannot** be cancelled.

But in the fraction $\dfrac{a(x + b)}{ac}$, a **is** a factor of the top expression, and also of the bottom expression. So the a's **can** be cancelled, giving $\dfrac{x + b}{c}$.

B7 Simplify these where possible.

If it is not possible, write 'cannot be simplified'.

(a) $\dfrac{xa}{xy}$ (b) $\dfrac{x+a}{x+y}$ (c) $\dfrac{xa}{x}$ (d) $\dfrac{x+a}{x}$ (e) $\dfrac{6}{x+3}$

B8 Simplify these where possible.
If it is not possible, write 'cannot be simplified'.

(a) $\dfrac{a+b}{a}$ (b) $\dfrac{a(b+c)}{b}$ (c) $\dfrac{ab}{a(x+y)}$ (d) $\dfrac{x^2}{2xy}$ (e) $\dfrac{x^2}{2x+y}$

(f) $\dfrac{x^2}{x(2+y)}$ (g) $\dfrac{ab}{a+b}$ (h) $\dfrac{3x+2}{x+1}$ (i) $\dfrac{4x}{2x+3}$ (j) $\dfrac{6x}{2(x+1)}$

B9 Which of these simplifications are correct, and which are wrong?

(a) $\dfrac{x^2}{5x+a} = \dfrac{x}{5+a}$ (b) $\dfrac{a^2b+c}{ab^2} = \dfrac{a+c}{b}$

(c) $\dfrac{n(n+2)}{3n^2} = \dfrac{n+2}{3n}$ (d) $\dfrac{n^2+2}{3n} = \dfrac{n+2}{3}$

C The reciprocal of a fraction

The **reciprocal** of a number is $\dfrac{1}{\text{the number}}$.

For example, the reciprocal of 5 is $\frac{1}{5}$ or 0·2.

When you multiply a number by its reciprocal, the result is 1.

$$5 \times \tfrac{1}{5} = 1 \qquad 4 \times \tfrac{1}{4} = 1 \qquad 52 \times \tfrac{1}{52} = 1$$

This means that the reciprocal of $\frac{1}{5}$ is 5, and so on.

C1 Write down (as a fraction or whole number) the reciprocal of

(a) 3   (b) $\frac{1}{4}$ (c) $\frac{1}{100}$ (d) 80   (e) 0·1   (f) 0·5

C2 The reciprocal of $\frac{2}{3}$ is the fraction which you have to multiply $\frac{2}{3}$ by to get 1.

$$\tfrac{2}{3} \times \tfrac{\cdots}{\cdots} = 1$$

What is the reciprocal of $\frac{2}{3}$?

The reciprocal of $\frac{2}{3}$ must be $\frac{3}{2}$, because $\frac{2}{3} \times \frac{3}{2} = \frac{6}{6} = 1$.

C3 What is the reciprocal of $\frac{3}{8}$? ($\frac{3}{8} \times \frac{\cdots}{\cdots} = 1$.)

C4 Write down the reciprocal of (a) $\frac{5}{9}$ (b) $\frac{3}{10}$ (c) $\frac{7}{5}$

To find the reciprocal of a fraction, you 'turn it upside down'.

So the reciprocal of $\frac{a}{b}$ is $\frac{b}{a}$, the reciprocal of $\frac{x}{x-y}$ is $\frac{x-y}{x}$, and so on.

C5 Write down the reciprocal of each of these.

(a) $\frac{pq}{r}$ (b) $\frac{x}{2}$ (c) $\frac{a}{b+c}$ (d) $2ab$ (e) $\frac{1}{4\pi}$ (f) $\frac{x(2-y)}{3a^2}$

C6 If an object is situated u m from a lens, and the lens makes an image on a screen v m from the lens, then the focal length f m of the lens can be obtained from the formula $f = \dfrac{uv}{u+v}$.

The power of the lens is measured in dioptres, and if the power is p dioptres then $p = \dfrac{1}{f}$. Write a formula for p in terms of u and v.

D Division

Dividing something by 5 is the same as finding $\frac{1}{5}$ of it. $30 \div 5 = \frac{1}{5}$ of 30	Finding $\frac{1}{5}$ of something is the same as multiplying it by $\frac{1}{5}$. $\frac{1}{5}$ of $30 = 30 \times \frac{1}{5}$	So dividing by 5 and multiplying by $\frac{1}{5}$ are the same. $30 \div 5 = 30 \times \frac{1}{5}$

The general rule is this: **dividing by a number is equivalent to multiplying by its reciprocal.**

This rule also works when we have to divide by a fraction.

For example, '$\div \frac{1}{2}$' is equivalent to '$\times 2$'.

You can see that this is true if you think of '$3 \div \frac{1}{2}$', for example, as 'how many $\frac{1}{2}$'s in 3?' The answer is 6, or 3×2.

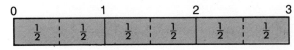

D1 (a) How many $\frac{1}{4}$-hours are there in 5 hours?

(b) Write the calculation as a division: $5 \div \frac{1}{4} = \ldots$

D2 Calculate these.

(a) $4 \div \frac{1}{3}$ (b) $7 \div \frac{1}{5}$ (c) $\frac{1}{2} \div \frac{1}{4}$ (d) $\frac{1}{3} \div \frac{1}{24}$ (e) $1 \div \frac{1}{9}$

The reciprocal of $\frac{2}{3}$ is $\frac{3}{2}$. So dividing by $\frac{2}{3}$ is equivalent to multiplying by $\frac{3}{2}$.

For example, $\frac{7}{8} \div \frac{2}{3} = \frac{7}{8} \times \frac{3}{2} = \frac{21}{16}$.

D3 Calculate these. Simplify the result if possible.

(a) $\frac{4}{5} \div \frac{2}{7}$ (b) $\frac{1}{4} \div \frac{3}{8}$ (c) $\frac{2}{5} \div \frac{2}{3}$ (d) $\frac{7}{8} \div \frac{5}{6}$

(e) $\dfrac{\frac{5}{8}}{\frac{2}{3}}$ (This means the same as $\frac{5}{8} \div \frac{2}{3}$.)   (f) $\dfrac{\frac{4}{5}}{\frac{2}{3}}$

Division involving algebraic fractions follows the rule.

For example, $\dfrac{a^2}{b} \div \dfrac{a}{c} = \dfrac{a^2}{b} \times \dfrac{c}{a} = \dfrac{\cancel{a}^{\,a}}{b} \times \dfrac{c}{\cancel{a}^{\,1}} = \dfrac{ac}{b}$

D4 Write each of these as a single algebraic fraction.
Simplify where possible.

(a) $\dfrac{p}{q} \div \dfrac{r}{s}$ (b) $\dfrac{p}{3} \div \dfrac{x}{2}$ (c) $\dfrac{a}{8} \div \dfrac{b}{4}$ (d) $\dfrac{a}{b^2} \div \dfrac{a^2}{c}$

(e) $\dfrac{3f}{g^2} \div \dfrac{h}{6g}$ (f) $\dfrac{m}{n} \div \dfrac{m^2}{n^2}$ (g) $\dfrac{a}{b} \div x$ (Remember $x = \frac{x}{1}$.)

(h) $\dfrac{5a}{b^2} \div b$ (i) $\dfrac{6a^2}{b} \div ab^2$ (j) $\dfrac{mv^2}{r} \div \dfrac{2r}{a}$ (k) $\dfrac{x}{a+b} \div \dfrac{b}{x+y}$

D5 (a) Calculate   (i) $\dfrac{\left(\frac{24}{6}\right)}{3}$ (ii) $\dfrac{24}{\left(\frac{6}{3}\right)}$

(b) Write as a single fraction

(i) $\dfrac{\left(\frac{a}{b}\right)}{c}$ (This means $\frac{a}{b} \div c$.)   (ii) $\dfrac{a}{\left(\frac{b}{c}\right)}$ (This means $a \div \frac{b}{c}$.)

D6 Write each of these as a single fraction.

(a) $\dfrac{\left(\frac{p}{2}\right)}{x}$ (b) $\dfrac{p}{\left(\frac{2}{x}\right)}$ (c) $\dfrac{\left(\frac{a}{b}\right)}{a}$ (d) $\dfrac{a}{\left(\frac{b}{a}\right)}$ (e) $\dfrac{\left(\frac{a}{x}\right)}{\left(\frac{x}{a}\right)}$ (f) $\dfrac{\left(\frac{a}{b}\right)}{\left(\frac{a}{b}\right)^2}$

39

6 Vectors

A Vector addition and subtraction

Let A and B be two fixed points on a grid.

The vector $\overrightarrow{AB}$ has a definite position on the grid, from point A to point B.

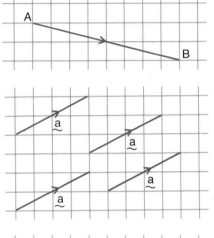

We often use a single small letter with a squiggle to stand for a vector.

For example, we could let $\underset{\sim}{a}$ stand for $\begin{bmatrix} 4 \\ 2 \end{bmatrix}$.

It does not matter where the vector is on the grid. If it is $\begin{bmatrix} 4 \\ 2 \end{bmatrix}$, it is $\underset{\sim}{a}$.

Let $\underset{\sim}{b} = \begin{bmatrix} 1 \\ 3 \end{bmatrix}$. We can add $\underset{\sim}{a}$ and $\underset{\sim}{b}$ by joining them end to end, as shown on the right. The result is the **vector sum** of $\underset{\sim}{a}$ and $\underset{\sim}{b}$.

$$\underset{\sim}{a} + \underset{\sim}{b} = \begin{bmatrix} 4 \\ 2 \end{bmatrix} + \begin{bmatrix} 1 \\ 3 \end{bmatrix} = \begin{bmatrix} 5 \\ 5 \end{bmatrix}.$$

A1 The vectors $\underset{\sim}{r}, \underset{\sim}{s}, \underset{\sim}{t}$ and $\underset{\sim}{u}$ are shown in the diagram on the right.

Write each of these as a column vector.

(a) $\underset{\sim}{r} + \underset{\sim}{s}$ (b) $\underset{\sim}{t} + \underset{\sim}{u}$

(c) $\underset{\sim}{r} + \underset{\sim}{u}$ (d) $\underset{\sim}{s} + \underset{\sim}{t}$

(e) $\underset{\sim}{r} + \underset{\sim}{t}$ (f) $\underset{\sim}{s} + \underset{\sim}{u}$

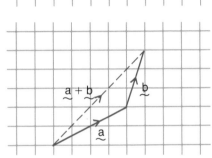

The **inverse** of a vector $\underset{\sim}{v}$ is the same length as $\underset{\sim}{v}$ but in the opposite direction to $\underset{\sim}{v}$.

The inverse of $\underset{\sim}{v}$ is written $^-\underset{\sim}{v}$.

For example, if $\underset{\sim}{v} = \begin{bmatrix} ^-4 \\ 3 \end{bmatrix}$, then $^-\underset{\sim}{v} = \begin{bmatrix} 4 \\ ^-3 \end{bmatrix}$.

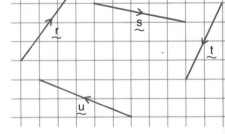
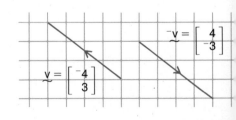

40

Subtracting vectors

With ordinary numbers, 'subtract 3' is the same as 'add $^-3$'.

Similarly with vectors, 'subtract $\underset{\sim}{a}$' is the same as 'add $^-\underset{\sim}{a}$'.

Suppose $\underset{\sim}{r} = \begin{bmatrix} 7 \\ 2 \end{bmatrix}$ and $\underset{\sim}{s} = \begin{bmatrix} 1 \\ 4 \end{bmatrix}$.

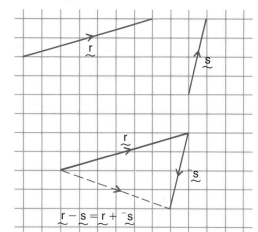

The diagram on the right shows $\underset{\sim}{r} - \underset{\sim}{s}$, which is the same as $\underset{\sim}{r} + {}^-\underset{\sim}{s}$.

$$\underset{\sim}{r} - \underset{\sim}{s} = \underset{\sim}{r} + {}^-\underset{\sim}{s} = \begin{bmatrix} 7 \\ 2 \end{bmatrix} + \begin{bmatrix} ^-1 \\ ^-4 \end{bmatrix}$$

$$= \begin{bmatrix} 6 \\ ^-2 \end{bmatrix}$$

A2 Let $\underset{\sim}{a} = \begin{bmatrix} 2 \\ 5 \end{bmatrix}$ and $\underset{\sim}{b} = \begin{bmatrix} 4 \\ 2 \end{bmatrix}$.

   (a) Draw a diagram showing $\underset{\sim}{a}$ and $^-\underset{\sim}{b}$ added together to give $\underset{\sim}{a} + {}^-\underset{\sim}{b}$ or $\underset{\sim}{a} - \underset{\sim}{b}$.

   (b) Write down $\underset{\sim}{a} - \underset{\sim}{b}$ as a column vector.

A3 Do the same as in question A2 for $\underset{\sim}{a} = \begin{bmatrix} ^-3 \\ 4 \end{bmatrix}$ and $\underset{\sim}{b} = \begin{bmatrix} 7 \\ ^-2 \end{bmatrix}$.

A4 If $\underset{\sim}{u} = \begin{bmatrix} 7 \\ 3 \end{bmatrix}$, $\underset{\sim}{v} = \begin{bmatrix} ^-6 \\ 2 \end{bmatrix}$ and $\underset{\sim}{w} = \begin{bmatrix} 4 \\ ^-5 \end{bmatrix}$, calculate

   (a) $\underset{\sim}{u} - \underset{\sim}{v}$ (b) $\underset{\sim}{v} - \underset{\sim}{u}$ (c) $\underset{\sim}{u} - \underset{\sim}{w}$ (d) $\underset{\sim}{w} - \underset{\sim}{u}$

   (e) $\underset{\sim}{v} - \underset{\sim}{w}$ (f) $\underset{\sim}{w} - \underset{\sim}{v}$

To calculate, for example, $\begin{bmatrix} 5 \\ 2 \end{bmatrix} - \begin{bmatrix} 6 \\ ^-3 \end{bmatrix}$,

you can **either** add the inverse of $\begin{bmatrix} 6 \\ ^-3 \end{bmatrix}$, like this: $\begin{bmatrix} 5 \\ 2 \end{bmatrix} + \begin{bmatrix} ^-6 \\ 3 \end{bmatrix} = \begin{bmatrix} ^-1 \\ 5 \end{bmatrix}$

or you can subtract directly, like this: $\begin{bmatrix} 5 \\ 2 \end{bmatrix} - \begin{bmatrix} 6 \\ ^-3 \end{bmatrix} = \begin{bmatrix} ^-1 \\ 5 \end{bmatrix}$ ⟵ 5−6=$^-$1

⟵ 2−$^-$3=5

If you decide to subtract, be careful when you subtract a negative number.

A5 Calculate these.

(a) $\begin{bmatrix} -2 \\ 4 \end{bmatrix} - \begin{bmatrix} 1 \\ -2 \end{bmatrix}$ (b) $\begin{bmatrix} 3 \\ -8 \end{bmatrix} - \begin{bmatrix} -2 \\ 3 \end{bmatrix}$ (c) $\begin{bmatrix} -5 \\ 1 \end{bmatrix} + \begin{bmatrix} -2 \\ -7 \end{bmatrix}$

(d) $\begin{bmatrix} 0 \\ 3 \end{bmatrix} - \begin{bmatrix} -2 \\ -1 \end{bmatrix}$ (e) $\begin{bmatrix} 4 \\ 0 \end{bmatrix} + \begin{bmatrix} -8 \\ -5 \end{bmatrix}$ (f) $\begin{bmatrix} -6 \\ -1 \end{bmatrix} - \begin{bmatrix} -9 \\ -5 \end{bmatrix}$

B Multiples of a vector

$3\underline{a}$ means a vector 3 times as long as $\underline{a}$ and in the same direction as $\underline{a}$.

For example, if $\underline{a} = \begin{bmatrix} 4 \\ 2 \end{bmatrix}$ then $3\underline{a} = \begin{bmatrix} 12 \\ 6 \end{bmatrix}$.

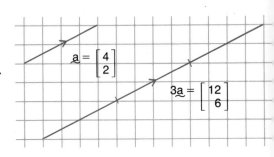

B1 If $\underline{u} = \begin{bmatrix} 4 \\ 5 \end{bmatrix}$ and $\underline{v} = \begin{bmatrix} -2 \\ 7 \end{bmatrix}$, calculate (a) $6\underline{u}$ (b) $4\underline{v}$

Let $\underline{a} = \begin{bmatrix} 4 \\ 2 \end{bmatrix}$. If we multiply $\underline{a}$ by $^{-}3$, we get $^{-}3\underline{a} = \begin{bmatrix} -12 \\ -6 \end{bmatrix}$.

$^{-}3\underline{a}$ is 3 times as long as $\underline{a}$, but in the opposite direction to $\underline{a}$.

We can also think of $^{-}3\underline{a}$ as $3(^{-}\underline{a})$.

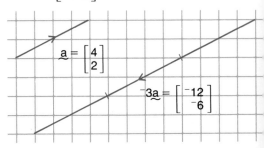

B2 Let $\underline{b} = \begin{bmatrix} -2 \\ 1 \end{bmatrix}$.

Draw the vectors $\underline{b}$, $2\underline{b}$ and $^{-}3\underline{b}$.

B3 If $\underline{r} = \begin{bmatrix} -4 \\ -5 \end{bmatrix}$, calculate (a) $6\underline{r}$ (b) $^{-}4\underline{r}$

B4 Calculate these.

(a) $2 \begin{bmatrix} -5 \\ 3 \end{bmatrix}$ (2 × the vector)   (b) $^{-}5 \begin{bmatrix} 4 \\ -6 \end{bmatrix}$ (c) $^{-}1 \cdot 5 \begin{bmatrix} -3 \\ 8 \end{bmatrix}$

C Linear sums

Suppose the vector $\underset{\sim}{u}$ is $\begin{bmatrix} 2 \\ 1 \end{bmatrix}$ and $\underset{\sim}{v}$ is $\begin{bmatrix} 1 \\ 3 \end{bmatrix}$.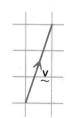

We can use these two vectors to 'generate' other vectors, by adding together multiples of $\underset{\sim}{u}$ and $\underset{\sim}{v}$.

This diagram shows the vector $\underset{\sim}{w}$, which is generated by adding $3\underset{\sim}{u}$ and $2\underset{\sim}{v}$.

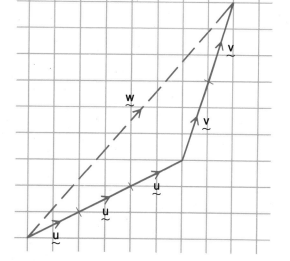

$$\underset{\sim}{w} = 3\underset{\sim}{u} + 2\underset{\sim}{v}$$

$$= 3\begin{bmatrix} 2 \\ 1 \end{bmatrix} + 2\begin{bmatrix} 1 \\ 3 \end{bmatrix}$$

$$= \begin{bmatrix} 6 \\ 3 \end{bmatrix} + \begin{bmatrix} 2 \\ 6 \end{bmatrix}$$

$$= \begin{bmatrix} 8 \\ 9 \end{bmatrix}$$

We say $\underset{\sim}{w}$ is a **linear sum** of $\underset{\sim}{u}$ and $\underset{\sim}{v}$.

A linear sum of $\underset{\sim}{u}$ and $\underset{\sim}{v}$ is any vector of the form $a\underset{\sim}{u} + b\underset{\sim}{v}$, where a and b are numbers.

C1 Calculate these linear sums of $\underset{\sim}{u}$ and $\underset{\sim}{v}$.

(a) $2\underset{\sim}{u} + \underset{\sim}{v}$ (b) $2\underset{\sim}{u} + 3\underset{\sim}{v}$ (c) $\underset{\sim}{u} + 4\underset{\sim}{v}$ (d) $5\underset{\sim}{u} + 5\underset{\sim}{v}$

The numbers a and b in the linear sum $a\underset{\sim}{u} + b\underset{\sim}{v}$ can be negative. For example, $3\underset{\sim}{u} + {}^-2\underset{\sim}{v}$ is a linear sum of $\underset{\sim}{u}$ and $\underset{\sim}{v}$; it can also be written $3\underset{\sim}{u} - 2\underset{\sim}{v}$.

We calculate $3\underset{\sim}{u} - 2\underset{\sim}{v}$ like this.

$$3\underset{\sim}{u} - 2\underset{\sim}{v}$$

$$= 3\begin{bmatrix} 2 \\ 1 \end{bmatrix} - 2\begin{bmatrix} 1 \\ 3 \end{bmatrix}$$

$$= \begin{bmatrix} 6 \\ 3 \end{bmatrix} - \begin{bmatrix} 2 \\ 6 \end{bmatrix} = \begin{bmatrix} 4 \\ -3 \end{bmatrix}$$

C2 Calculate these linear sums of $\underset{\sim}{u}$ and $\underset{\sim}{v}$.

(a) $4\underset{\sim}{u} - \underset{\sim}{v}$ (b) $\underset{\sim}{u} - 2\underset{\sim}{v}$ (c) $4\underset{\sim}{u} - 3\underset{\sim}{v}$ (d) $^-2\underset{\sim}{u} - 3\underset{\sim}{v}$

(e) $5\underset{\sim}{u} - 4\underset{\sim}{v}$ (f) $^-\underset{\sim}{u} - \underset{\sim}{v}$ (g) $^-3\underset{\sim}{u} + 2\underset{\sim}{v}$ (h) $^-5\underset{\sim}{u} - 2\underset{\sim}{v}$

You have to be careful with signs ($+$ and $-$) when you calculate linear sums.

Worked example

If $p = \begin{bmatrix} -3 \\ 2 \end{bmatrix}$ and $q = \begin{bmatrix} 4 \\ -5 \end{bmatrix}$, calculate $2p - 3q$.

$$2p - 3q = 2\begin{bmatrix} -3 \\ 2 \end{bmatrix} - 3\begin{bmatrix} 4 \\ -5 \end{bmatrix}$$

$$\begin{bmatrix} -6 \\ 4 \end{bmatrix} - \begin{bmatrix} 12 \\ -15 \end{bmatrix} = \begin{bmatrix} -18 \\ 19 \end{bmatrix}$$

$-6 - 12 = -18$

$4 - -15 = 4 + 15 = 19$

This is $2p$.   This is $3q$.

C3 If $r = \begin{bmatrix} 3 \\ -4 \end{bmatrix}$ and $s = \begin{bmatrix} -2 \\ 5 \end{bmatrix}$, calculate these.

(a) $r - s$ (b) $2r - s$ (c) $r - 2s$ (d) $3r - 2s$ (e) $-4r + 5s$

C4 If $c = \begin{bmatrix} 3 \\ -2 \end{bmatrix}$ and $d = \begin{bmatrix} -1 \\ -4 \end{bmatrix}$, calculate these.

(a) $c + d$ (b) $-2c + d$ (c) $3c - d$ (d) $5c - 2d$ (e) $c - 3d$

Reversing the process

Let u be $\begin{bmatrix} 2 \\ 1 \end{bmatrix}$ and v be $\begin{bmatrix} 1 \\ 3 \end{bmatrix}$ (as on the previous page).

We have seen how to calculate a linear sum $au + bv$ when we are given the numbers a and b.

Here is an example of the 'reverse' problem.

What are the numbers a and b if the linear sum $au + bv$ is equal to $\begin{bmatrix} 9 \\ 7 \end{bmatrix}$?

We can think about this problem geometrically.

How can we make $\begin{bmatrix} 9 \\ 7 \end{bmatrix}$ . . .   . . . by adding together multiples of $\begin{bmatrix} 2 \\ 1 \end{bmatrix}$ and $\begin{bmatrix} 1 \\ 3 \end{bmatrix}$?

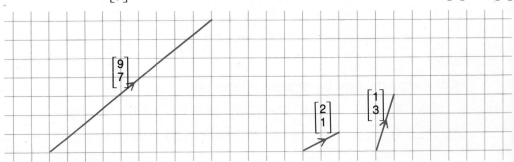

By trial and error we can get this solution.

$$\begin{bmatrix} 9 \\ 7 \end{bmatrix} = 4\underset{\sim}{u} + \underset{\sim}{v}$$

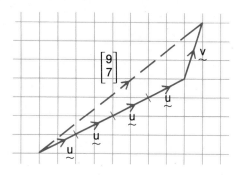

C5 (a) On squared paper, draw the vector $\begin{bmatrix} 10 \\ 15 \end{bmatrix}$.

(b) Find a linear sum of $\underset{\sim}{u}$ and $\underset{\sim}{v}$ which is equal to $\begin{bmatrix} 10 \\ 15 \end{bmatrix}$.

Write it in the form $\dots \underset{\sim}{u} + \dots \underset{\sim}{v}$. ($\underset{\sim}{u}$ and $\underset{\sim}{v}$ are the same as before.)

C6 Let $\underset{\sim}{p}$ be $\begin{bmatrix} 3 \\ 2 \end{bmatrix}$ and $\underset{\sim}{q}$ be $\begin{bmatrix} 5 \\ 1 \end{bmatrix}$.

Draw the vector $\underset{\sim}{r} = \begin{bmatrix} 21 \\ 7 \end{bmatrix}$ on squared paper. Find a linear sum of $\underset{\sim}{p}$ and $\underset{\sim}{q}$ which is equal to $\underset{\sim}{r}$.

C7 Let $\underset{\sim}{c}$ be $\begin{bmatrix} 2 \\ 3 \end{bmatrix}$ and $\underset{\sim}{d}$ be $\begin{bmatrix} 4 \\ 1 \end{bmatrix}$.

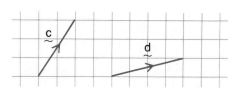

Draw the vector $\underset{\sim}{e} = \begin{bmatrix} 4 \\ 11 \end{bmatrix}$ on squared paper. Find a linear sum of $\underset{\sim}{c}$ and $\underset{\sim}{d}$ which is equal to $\underset{\sim}{e}$. (One of the multiples of $\underset{\sim}{c}$ or $\underset{\sim}{d}$ is negative.)

C8 Let $\underset{\sim}{f}$ be $\begin{bmatrix} -2 \\ 2 \end{bmatrix}$ and $\underset{\sim}{g}$ be $\begin{bmatrix} 2 \\ 1 \end{bmatrix}$.

(a) Draw vector $\underset{\sim}{h} = \begin{bmatrix} -12 \\ 6 \end{bmatrix}$ on squared paper. Find a linear sum of $\underset{\sim}{f}$ and $\underset{\sim}{g}$ which is equal to $\underset{\sim}{e}$.

(b) Write down a linear sum of $\underset{\sim}{f}$ and $\underset{\sim}{g}$ which is equal to each of these.

(i) $\begin{bmatrix} -24 \\ 12 \end{bmatrix}$ (ii) $\begin{bmatrix} -120 \\ 60 \end{bmatrix}$ (iii) $\begin{bmatrix} 12 \\ -6 \end{bmatrix}$ (iv) $\begin{bmatrix} 6 \\ -3 \end{bmatrix}$

D Using algebra

Suppose we have two vectors $\underline{u}$ and $\underline{v}$, and a third vector $\underline{w}$.
Suppose we find a linear sum of $\underline{u}$ and $\underline{v}$ which is equal to $\underline{w}$.
For example, it may turn out that $\underline{w}$ is equal to $3\underline{u} + 5\underline{v}$.
We then say we have **expressed $\underline{w}$ as a linear sum of $\underline{u}$ and $\underline{v}$**.

So far we have used diagrams to express one vector as a linear sum of
two others. But the problem can also be solved by algebra.

Worked example

Let $\underline{u} = \begin{bmatrix} 2 \\ 5 \end{bmatrix}$, $\underline{v} = \begin{bmatrix} 1 \\ 3 \end{bmatrix}$ and $\underline{w} = \begin{bmatrix} 9 \\ 25 \end{bmatrix}$

Express $\underline{w}$ as a linear sum of $\underline{u}$ and $\underline{v}$.

We are trying to find two numbers a and b for which $a\underline{u} + b\underline{v}$ is equal to $\underline{w}$.

$$\text{So } a\begin{bmatrix} 2 \\ 5 \end{bmatrix} + b\begin{bmatrix} 1 \\ 3 \end{bmatrix} = \begin{bmatrix} 9 \\ 25 \end{bmatrix}$$

$$\text{So } \begin{bmatrix} 2a \\ 5a \end{bmatrix} + \begin{bmatrix} b \\ 3b \end{bmatrix} = \begin{bmatrix} 9 \\ 25 \end{bmatrix}$$

This is a times $\begin{bmatrix} 2 \\ 5 \end{bmatrix}$.   This is b times $\begin{bmatrix} 1 \\ 3 \end{bmatrix}$.

It follows that $2a + b = 9$
and $5a + 3b = 25$

We can solve these equations in the usual way, by eliminating
one of the letters.

D1 (a) Solve the equations in the example above to find a and b.

(b) Write the final answer to the problem in the form $\underline{w} = \ldots \underline{u} + \ldots \underline{v}$.

(c) Draw a diagram showing $\underline{w}$ as a linear sum of $\underline{u}$ and $\underline{v}$.

D2 Let $\underline{p} = \begin{bmatrix} 4 \\ 1 \end{bmatrix}$, $\underline{q} = \begin{bmatrix} 2 \\ 5 \end{bmatrix}$ and $\underline{r} = \begin{bmatrix} 4 \\ 19 \end{bmatrix}$.

Express $\underline{r}$ as a linear sum of $\underline{p}$ and $\underline{q}$.

Start by writing $a\begin{bmatrix} 4 \\ 1 \end{bmatrix} + b\begin{bmatrix} 2 \\ 5 \end{bmatrix} = \begin{bmatrix} 4 \\ 19 \end{bmatrix}$.

Write two equations for a and b and solve them.

D3 Let $\underline{c} = \begin{bmatrix} 1 \\ 5 \end{bmatrix}$, $\underline{d} = \begin{bmatrix} -2 \\ 3 \end{bmatrix}$ and $\underline{e} = \begin{bmatrix} -1 \\ 21 \end{bmatrix}$.

Express $\underline{e}$ as a linear sum of $\underline{c}$ and $\underline{d}$.

D4 Let $\underset{\sim}{u} = \begin{bmatrix} 2 \\ 1 \end{bmatrix}$, $\underset{\sim}{v} = \begin{bmatrix} 6 \\ 3 \end{bmatrix}$ and $\underset{\sim}{w} = \begin{bmatrix} 10 \\ 8 \end{bmatrix}$.

   (a) See what happens when you try to express $\underset{\sim}{w}$ as a linear sum of $\underset{\sim}{u}$ and $\underset{\sim}{v}$.

   (b) Draw a diagram showing $\underset{\sim}{u}$, $\underset{\sim}{v}$ and $\underset{\sim}{w}$ and use it to explain the result in part (a).

D5 Let $\underset{\sim}{p} = \begin{bmatrix} 3 \\ 2 \end{bmatrix}$, $\underset{\sim}{q} = \begin{bmatrix} 6 \\ 4 \end{bmatrix}$ and $\underset{\sim}{r} = \begin{bmatrix} 15 \\ 10 \end{bmatrix}$.

   (a) See what happens when you try to express $\underset{\sim}{r}$ as a linear sum of $\underset{\sim}{p}$ and $\underset{\sim}{q}$.

   (b) Draw a diagram and explain the result in part (a).

D6 Let $\underset{\sim}{c} = \begin{bmatrix} 4 \\ 3 \end{bmatrix}$, $\underset{\sim}{d} = \begin{bmatrix} 1 \\ 2 \end{bmatrix}$, and $\underset{\sim}{e} = \begin{bmatrix} 10 \\ 5 \end{bmatrix}$.

   (a) Express $\underset{\sim}{e}$ in terms of $\underset{\sim}{c}$ and $\underset{\sim}{d}$.

   (b) Use your answer to part (a) to express $\underset{\sim}{c}$ in terms of $\underset{\sim}{d}$ and $\underset{\sim}{e}$. (Do not solve another pair of equations.)

   (c) Use your answer to part (a) to express $\underset{\sim}{d}$ in terms of $\underset{\sim}{c}$ and $\underset{\sim}{e}$.

D7 A laboratory stores acid in two different concentrations, 'strong' and 'weak'.

   'Strong' acid is 80% pure acid and 20% water, by volume. One litre of 'strong' acid can be represented by the vector $\begin{bmatrix} 0 \cdot 8 \\ 0 \cdot 2 \end{bmatrix}$.

   'Weak' acid is 40% pure acid and 60% water, by volume. One litre of 'weak' acid can be represented by the vector $\begin{bmatrix} 0 \cdot 4 \\ 0 \cdot 6 \end{bmatrix}$.

   (a) A chemist needs a mixture consisting of 5 litres of pure acid and 5 litres of water. This mixture can be represented by the vector $\begin{bmatrix} 5 \\ 5 \end{bmatrix}$.
   The chemist gets the mixture by mixing together a litres of 'strong' acid and b litres of 'weak'.

   Write down an equation connecting the three vectors, and solve it.

   (b) Another chemist needs a mixture consisting of 3 litres of pure acid and 7 litres of water.
   Write down another equation and solve it. Use the result to explain why the second chemist cannot make her mixture from the 'strong' and 'weak' acids.

1 Selections and arrangements

1.1 The Whistlestop European Tour includes one day in London.
In the morning, tourists can visit either St Paul's or Westminster Abbey.
In the afternoon, they can go to the Science Museum, the British Museum
or the Natural History Museum.
In the evening, they can go to Highgate Cemetery, Kensal Green Cemetery
or Battersea Power Station.

How many different one-day programmes can be selected?

1.2 Rowena wants a hi-fi set, consisting of an amplifier, a record
deck and a pair of speakers.
She has saved up £200 to spend on equipment.
Here are the prices of the things she could buy.

Amplifiers		Record decks		Speakers (pair)	
Model A	£85	Model P	£65	Model X	£40
Model B	£110	Model Q	£75	Model Y	£65
Model C	£95	Model R	£50	Model Z	£70
Model D	£140	Model S	£90		
		Model T	£80		

Draw a tree diagram showing all the different selections she could
make.

1.3 A political party has to choose a leader and a deputy leader.
There are four candidates for the leadership: A, B, C and D.
A and B are also candidates for the deputy leadership, but
in addition there are two others, X and Y.

Draw a tree diagram to show all the different ways in which
the two jobs can be filled. (The same person is not allowed to be
both leader and deputy leader.)

1.4 A box contains a 1p piece, a 2p piece, a 5p piece and a 10p piece.
If some coins are taken from the box, we can use a binary code to
show what is taken. So, for example, 1001 means '1p taken,
2p not taken, 5p not taken, 10p taken'.

(a) How many different codes are there, excluding 0000?

(b) A second box contains a £5 note, a £10 note, a £20 note and a £50 note.
If you take coins (at least one) from the first box and notes (at least
one) from the second, how many different selections can you make?

2 Enlargement and volume

2.1 Box B is an enlargement of box A.

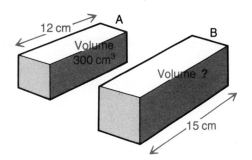

(a) Calculate the scale factor of the enlargement from A to B.

(b) Calculate the volume factor of the enlargement.

(c) Calculate the volume of box B, to the nearest cm^3.

2.2 The area of cardboard used to make box A is $300\,\text{cm}^2$. Calculate the area used to make box B, to the nearest cm^2.

2.3 A bottle Y is a reduction of another bottle X.
Bottle X is 20 cm tall and has a volume of 150 ml.
Bottle Y is 14 cm tall.

(a) Calculate the volume of bottle Y.

(b) Roughly how many times can bottle Y be filled from bottle X?

3 Linear equations

3.1 Solve each of these pairs of equations.

(a) $3x + 2y = 19$
    $2x + 5y = 20$

(b) $2a - 3b = 11$
    $5a + 2b = 18$

3.2 Find the coordinates of the point of intersection of the lines whose equations are $5x - 3y = 6$ and $3x + 7y = 8$.

3.3 Last weekend three adults and five children visited the zoo.
The total cost of their entrance tickets was £23·70.
This weekend two adults and four children visited the zoo, and the total cost was £17·60.

Calculate the cost of an adult entrance ticket and of a child's entrance ticket.

3.4 Solve each of these pairs of equations, where possible.
If there is no solution, or infinitely many solutions, say so.

(a) $4p - 2q = 26$
    $3p + 5q = 39$

(b) $4p - 2q = 26$
    $6p - 3q = 36$

(c) $2x + 5y = 8$
    $6x + 15y = 24$

(d) $5x + 3y = 20$
    $2x + y = 20$

4 Angle relationships

4.1 The lines AB, AC and AD in this diagram are equal in length.

Calculate the angle marked a, explaining how you do it.

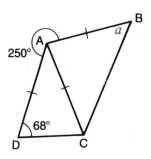

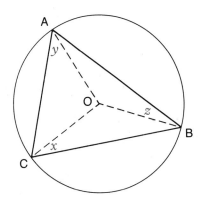

4.2 O is the centre of the circle in this diagram.

Explain why $x + y + z = 90°$.

4.3 (a) Calculate the exterior angle of a regular polygon with 40 sides.

(b) Calculate the interior angle.

(c) If each interior angle of a regular polygon is 168°, how many sides does the polygon have?

4.4 The lines AB, BC and CD in this diagram are equal in length.

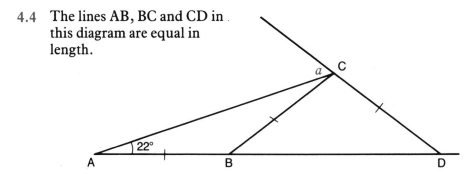

Calculate the angle marked a, explaining how you do it.

*4.5 The diagram for this question is the same as that for question 4.4, except that angle CAB is $x°$.

Explain why angle a must be $3x°$.

5 Algebraic fractions

5.1 Simplify these if possible.

(a) $\dfrac{m^2 n}{mn^2}$ (b) $\dfrac{3x^2 + a}{ax}$ (c) $\dfrac{12p^2 qr}{3q^2 r}$ (d) $a \times \left(\dfrac{x}{a}\right)^2$ (e) $\dfrac{x + a}{x - a}$

5.2 Write each of these as a single fraction. Simplify if possible.

(a) $\dfrac{3}{4} \div \dfrac{2}{3}$ (b) $\dfrac{3}{4} \div \dfrac{1}{x}$ (c) $\dfrac{m^2}{n} \div \dfrac{m}{n^2}$ (d) $\dfrac{ab^2}{c} \times \dfrac{c^2}{2a}$ (e) $\dfrac{a}{x + 1} \div \dfrac{3}{x + 1}$

(f) $\dfrac{ab}{c} \div \dfrac{a}{b}$ (g) $\dfrac{1}{\left(\dfrac{p}{q}\right)^2}$ (h) $\dfrac{4\pi r^3}{3} \div 4\pi r^2$ (i) $\dfrac{mgh}{\frac{1}{2} mv^2}$

6 Vectors

6.1 $\underset{\sim}{a}$, $\underset{\sim}{b}$ and $\underset{\sim}{c}$ are shown in this diagram.

Calculate each of these as a column vector.

(a) $\underset{\sim}{a} + \underset{\sim}{b}$ (b) $\underset{\sim}{a} - \underset{\sim}{b}$

(c) $4\underset{\sim}{b}$ (d) $^-3\underset{\sim}{c}$

(e) $3\underset{\sim}{a} + 2\underset{\sim}{b}$ (f) $2\underset{\sim}{b} - 5\underset{\sim}{c}$

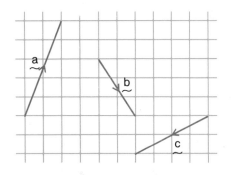

6.2 If $\underset{\sim}{u} = \begin{bmatrix} 3 \\ 1 \end{bmatrix}$, $\underset{\sim}{v} = \begin{bmatrix} 4 \\ 3 \end{bmatrix}$ and $\underset{\sim}{w} = \begin{bmatrix} 23 \\ 11 \end{bmatrix}$, express $\underset{\sim}{w}$ as

a linear sum of $\underset{\sim}{u}$ and $\underset{\sim}{v}$.

6.3 If $\underset{\sim}{a} = \begin{bmatrix} ^-1 \\ 3 \end{bmatrix}$, $\underset{\sim}{b} = \begin{bmatrix} 2 \\ 5 \end{bmatrix}$ and $\underset{\sim}{c} = \begin{bmatrix} 4 \\ 21 \end{bmatrix}$, express $\underset{\sim}{c}$ as

a linear sum of $\underset{\sim}{a}$ and $\underset{\sim}{b}$.

6.4 If $\underset{\sim}{x} = \begin{bmatrix} 3 \\ 2 \end{bmatrix}$, $\underset{\sim}{y} = \begin{bmatrix} 1 \\ 2 \end{bmatrix}$ and $\underset{\sim}{z} = \begin{bmatrix} 13 \\ 6 \end{bmatrix}$, express $\underset{\sim}{z}$ as

a linear sum of $\underset{\sim}{x}$ and $\underset{\sim}{y}$.

6.5 Explain why the vector $\begin{bmatrix} 20 \\ 25 \end{bmatrix}$ cannot be expressed as a

linear sum of $\begin{bmatrix} 2 \\ 3 \end{bmatrix}$ and $\begin{bmatrix} 8 \\ 12 \end{bmatrix}$.

M Miscellaneous

M1 The pair of equations $y = 5x + 8$ has no solution.
$$2y = ax + b$$

What can you say about the values of a and b?

M2 (a) Calculate the length of the line joining the points $(2 \cdot 5, 1 \cdot 3)$ and $(4 \cdot 5, 3 \cdot 3)$.

(b) Calculate the gradient of the line joining $(6 \cdot 6, 3 \cdot 8)$ and $(19 \cdot 1, 16 \cdot 3)$.

(c) Without drawing, how can you decide whether the line in (a) is parallel to the line in (b)?

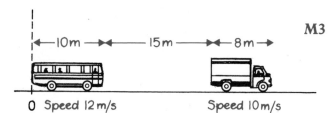

M3 A coach and a lorry are travelling in parallel lanes.

Time t is measured in seconds from the instant the picture was taken.

(a) Write an expression for the distance, in metres, of each of these from the point O at time t.

   (i) The back of the coach   (ii) The front of the coach
 (iii) The back of the lorry   (iv) The front of the lorry

(b) Write an equation which says that at time t the back of the coach just passes the front of the lorry, and solve the equation.

M4 The race track problem

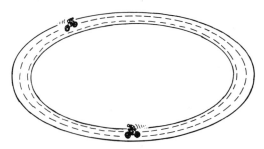

Two cyclists are riding round a circular race track, each with a constant speed and in the same direction.

One cyclist takes 25 seconds to go round once. The other takes 45 seconds.

How often will the faster cyclist overtake the other? (Work out the time between two overtakings.)

7 Sequences (1)

A 'Term-to-term' rules for sequences

Suppose you stand by the roadside and note down the number
of people (including the driver) in each car as it goes by.
You might get a list like this: 2, 1, 1, 3, 3, 2, 4, 1, 5, 2, 3, 4, 4, 1, 5, . . .

A list of numbers in a definite order is called a **sequence**.
There is no pattern in the sequence above, so you cannot work out
how it will continue. It is a **random sequence**.

The sequence you get when you start with 3 and then double each
time is a **rule-governed sequence**: 3, 6, 12, 24, 48, 96, 192, 384, . . .
This sequence can continue for ever.

A1 In each of these sequences there is a simple rule for going
from one number to the next.
Find the rule, and write down the next three numbers in
each sequence.

(a) 4, 7, 10, 13, 16, . . . (b) 1, 3, 9, 27, 81, . . .

(c) $1, \frac{1}{2}, \frac{1}{4}, \frac{1}{8}, \frac{1}{16}, \ldots$ (d) 0·8, 1·0, 1·2, 1·4, . . .

Each number in a sequence is called a **term** of the sequence.
In sequence (a) above, the 1st term is 4, the 2nd term is 7, and so on.

Often there is a simple rule for going from one term to the next.
In sequence (a) in question A1, the rule is 'add 3'. We will call
this rule the 'term-to-term' rule for the sequence.

A2 What is the term-to-term rule for each sequence in question A1?

When you know the term-to-term rule of a sequence, you can continue
the sequence by applying the rule again and again.
For example, if you want the 10th term of sequence (a) in question A1,
you start with the 1st term, 4, and then keep adding on 3.

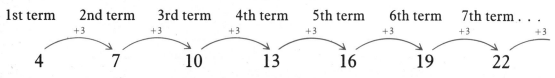

1st term	2nd term	3rd term	4th term	5th term	6th term	7th term . . .
+3	+3	+3	+3	+3	+3	+3
4	7	10	13	16	19	22

A3 (a) Starting with 4, how many times do you have to add 3
to get to the 7th term? (Be careful!)
(b) Starting with 4, how many times do you have to add 3
to get to the 16th term?

To get to the **10th** term in the sequence in question A3 you start with 4 and add on 3 **nine** times.

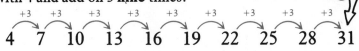

To get to the **16th** term you start with 4 and add on 3 **fifteen** times.

A4 (a) What is the term-to-term rule of this sequence?
2, 7, 12, 17, 22, 27, 32, . . .

(b) Starting with the 1st term, 2, how many times do you have to apply the term-to-term rule to get to the 20th term?

(c) What is the 20th term?

(d) What is the 50th term?

A5 In the 1st year at a new job, Stanley is paid a salary of £8400.
His salary goes up by £300 every year.
What is his salary in

(a) the 5th year   (b) the 12th year   (c) the 43rd year

A6 If the 1st year of Stanley's job was the year 1971, what was the 20th year?

B 'Position-to-term' rules

This is the sequence of **square numbers:**   1, 4, 9, 16, 25, . . .

This table shows the position of each square number in the sequence.

Position	1st	2nd	3rd	4th	5th	6th	7th	8th . . .
Term	1	4	9	16	25	36	49	64 . . .

There is a simple rule for going from **position** to **term:**
the 1st term is 1^2, the 2nd term is 2^2, the 3rd term is 3^2, and so on.
The 40th term will be $40^2 = 1600$.

A rule of this kind we will call a 'position-to-term' rule.

There is a term-to-term rule for the sequence of square numbers, but it is complicated, because the difference between each term and the next one changes.

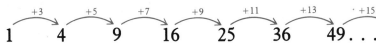

You could use this rule to work out, say, the 300th square number, but it is much easier to use the position-to-term rule.

B1 (a) What is the position-to-term rule of this sequence?
(b) What is the 100th term?

Position	1	2	3	4	5	6
Term	4	8	12	16	20	24

Here is a sequence which has both a simple term-to-term rule and a simple position-to-term rule.

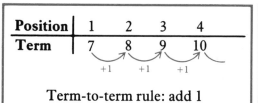

Position	1	2	3	4
Term	7	8	9	10

+1 +1 +1

Term-to-term rule: add 1

Position	1	2	3	4
Term	7	8	9	10

+6 +6 +6 +6

Position-to-term rule: add 6

B2 (a) What is the position-to-term rule for this sequence?

Positon	1	2	3	4	5	6	. . .
Term	5	10	15	20	25	30	. . .

(b) What is the 20th term of the sequence?

B3 (a) What is the position-to-term rule for this sequence?

Position	1	2	3	4	5	6	. . .
Term	4	5	6	7	8	9	. . .

(b) What is the 92nd term of the sequence?

B4 For each of these sequences, write down
(i) the term-to-term rule   (ii) the position-to-term rule

(a)

Position	1	2	3	4	5	6	7	. . .
Term	3	6	9	12	15	18	21	. . .

(b)

Position	1	2	3	4	5	6	7	. . .
Term	$\frac{1}{3}$	$\frac{2}{3}$	1	$1\frac{1}{3}$	$1\frac{2}{3}$	2	$2\frac{1}{3}$	. . .

B5 (a) What is position-to-term rule for this sequence?

Position	1	2	3	4	5	6	7	. . .
Term	1	8	27	64	125	216	343	. . .

(b) What is the 15th term of the sequence?

B6 The term-to-term rule for this sequence is a simple one.

Position	1	2	3	4	5	6	7	. . .
Term	7	11	15	19	23	27	31	. . .

The position-to-term rule is not so simple. It involves two operations.
(a) Can you find the position-to-term rule?
(b) Use it to work out the 100th term of the sequence.

55

C Arithmetic sequences

A sequence in which you go from term-to-term by **adding** or **subtracting** the same number each time is called an arithmetic (say arithmetic) sequence.

These are examples of arithmetic sequences.

(A)
Position	1	2	3	4	5	6	...
Term	7	11	15	19	23	27	...

Term-to-term rule: add 4

(B)
Position	1	2	3	4	5	...
Term	10	7	4	1	⁻2	...

Term-to-term rule: subtract 3

You can work out terms of sequences like these by deciding how many times you need to apply the term-to-term rule.

For example, suppose you want the 6th term of sequence A above. Starting with the 1st term, 7, you have to **add on 4** a total of 5 times to get the 6th term.

So altogether you have to add on 5×4, or **20**, to the first term, 7. So the 6th term is $7 + 20 = \mathbf{27}$.

> **C1** Calculate in a similar way these terms of sequence A.
> (a) the 10th   (b) the 20th   (c) the 51st   (d) the 103rd

We can use algebra to show how to calculate terms of sequence A.

Suppose we want to calculate the nth term of sequence A.

We start with the first term, 7, and we have to add 4 a total of $(n-1)$ times. (For the 6th term it was 5 times, and so on.)

So altogether we have to add on $(n-1) \times 4$, or $\mathbf{4(n-1)}$, to the 1st term.

So the nth term is $7 + 4(n-1)$
$$= 7 + 4n - 4$$
$$= 3 + 4n$$

This is the most useful way of writing the position-to-term rule.

(We can check that this formula works. For example, if n is 5, the formula says the 5th term is $3 + (4 \times 5) = 23$, which is correct.)

> **C2** (a) What is the **term-to-term** rule of this sequence?
>
> | Position | 1 | 2 | 3 | 4 | 5 | 6 | ... |
> |----------|---|----|----|----|----|----|-----|
> | Term | 8 | 14 | 20 | 26 | 32 | 38 | ... |
>
> (b) Work out a formula for the nth term.
>
> (c) Check that the formula gives the correct result when n is 5.

> **C3** Work out a formula for the nth term of this sequence.
>
> | Position | 1 | 2 | 3 | 4 | ... |
> |----------|---|---|----|----|-----|
> | Term | 5 | 8 | 11 | 14 | ... |

C4 Work out a formula for the nth term of each of these arithmetic sequences. Check each formula when n is 5.

(a)
Position	1	2	3	4	...
Term	9	14	19	24	...

(b)
Position	1	2	3	4	...
Term	3	10	17	24	...

In this arithmetic sequence, the term-to-term rule is 'subtract 3'.

Position	1	2	3	4	5	6	...
Term	10	7	4	1	⁻2	⁻5	...

To get the nth term, we start with the 1st term, 10, and **subtract 3** a total of $(n-1)$ times.

So altogether we have to subtract $(n-1) \times 3$, or $3(n-1)$, from the 1st term.

So the nth term is $10 - 3(n-1)$
$$= 10 - 3n + 3$$
$$= 13 - 3n.$$

C5 Check that the formula $13 - 3n$ is correct when n is 6.

C6 (a) What is the term-to-term rule of this sequence?

Position	1	2	3	4	5	6	...
Term	9	7	5	3	1	⁻1	...

(b) Work out a formula for the nth term of the sequence.

(c) Check that it gives the correct result when n is 6.

C7 Work out a formula for the nth term of each of these arithmetic sequences. Check by putting n equal to 5.

(a)
Position	1	2	3	4	...
Term	12	7	2	⁻3	...

(b)
Position	1	2	3	4	...
Term	18	14	10	6	...

(c)
Position	1	2	3	4	...
Term	5	7	9	11	...

(d)
Position	1	2	3	4	...
Term	⁻5	⁻1	3	7	...

C8 This pattern of short and tall houses continues along the odd-numbered side of a street.

Work out a formula for the number of the nth tall house.

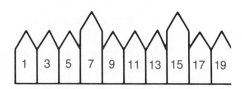

D Geometric sequences

The name **geometric sequence** is given to a sequence where you go from term to term by multiplying or dividing by the same number each time.

Here are two examples of geometric sequences.

(A)

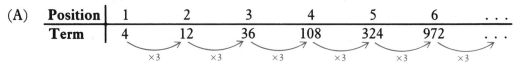

Position	1	2	3	4	5	6	. . .
Term	4	12	36	108	324	972	. . .

×3 ×3 ×3 ×3 ×3 ×3

The term-to-term rule is **multiply by 3**.

(B) In the sequence below, the term-to-term rule is **divide by 2**.
Dividing by 2 is the same as **multiplying by $\frac{1}{2}$**. We usually think of the term-to-term rule in a geometric sequence as **multiplying** by something rather than dividing.

Position	1	2	3	4	5	6	. . .
Term	80	40	20	10	5	$2\frac{1}{2}$	. . .

$×\frac{1}{2}$ $×\frac{1}{2}$ $×\frac{1}{2}$ $×\frac{1}{2}$ $×\frac{1}{2}$ $×\frac{1}{2}$

As with arithmetic sequences, we can calculate terms of a geometric sequence by starting with the first term and applying the term-to-term rule again and again. The only change is that we **multiply** again and again instead of adding or subtracting.

> **D1** Start with the first term, 4, of sequence A.
>
> (a) How many times do you multiply the first term by 3 to get the 8th term?
>
> (b) How many times do you multiply the first term by 3 to get the 17th term?

To get the 6th term of sequence A we work out $4 \times 3 \times 3 \times 3 \times 3 \times 3$
5 times

We can write this using powers, like this: 4×3^5.

> **D2** (a) Write the 8th term of sequence A in the form $4 \times 3^?$.
>
> (b) Do the same for the 17th term of sequence A.
>
> **D3** Write down a formula for the nth term of sequence A.
>
> **D4** The formula for the nth term of another sequence is $5 \times 2^{n-1}$.
> Work out
> (a) the 3rd term   (b) the 5th term   (c) the 6th term

D5 Find a formula for the nth term of each of these geometric sequences.

(a)

Position	1	2	3	4	. . .
Term	3	6	12	24	. . .

(b)

Position	1	2	3	4	. . .
Term	5	30	180	1080	. . .

D6 What do you get when you use the formulas you got in question D5 to work out the 1st term of each sequence?

D7 What is the first term of the sequence whose nth term is $8 \times 5^{n-1}$?

This geometric sequence starts with first term 6, and its term-to-term rule is multiply by 4.

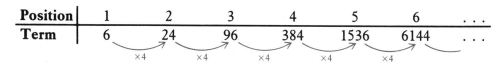

Position	1	2	3	4	5	6	
Term	6	24	96	384	1536	6144	. . .

The nth term of the sequence is $\underbrace{6 \times 4 \times 4 \times \ldots \times 4}_{(n-1)\ \text{times}} = 6 \times 4^{n-1}$

Now we see what happens when we use the formula $6 \times 4^{n-1}$ to find the 1st term. If we replace n in the formula by 1, we get 6×4^0.

But we know from the table that the first term is 6.
So 4^0 has to mean the same as 1, so that $6 \times 4^0 = 6 \times 1 = 6$.

Another way to see why 4^0 is 1 is to think of the sequence of powers of 4.

$4^1 \quad 4^2 \quad 4^3 \quad 4^4 \quad \ldots$

$4 \quad 16 \quad 64 \quad 256 \quad \ldots$

As you go from left to right, you multiply by 4 each time, and the power goes up by 1.

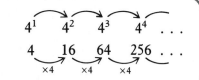

Now continue the pattern backwards. We **divide by 4** each time, and the power goes **down** by 1.

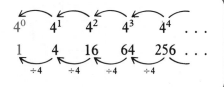

There is nothing special about 4. We could do the same with 2, or with **any** number. $a^0 = 1$ whatever the value of a.

59

E The triangle numbers

This sequence of triangular dot patterns give rise to the sequence of **triangle numbers**.

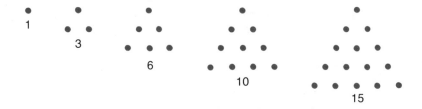

Position	1	2	3	4	5	6	...
Term	1	3	6	10	15	21	...

The 1st triangle number is 1.
The 2nd triangle number is 1 + 2.
The 3rd triangle number is 1 + 2 + 3, and so on.

Suppose we want to know the 50th triangle number. We could do 1 + 2 + 3 + 4 + ... up to 50, but perhaps there is a shorter way to work it out.

The next question suggests a method for finding the 10th triangle number. A similar method can be used to find any triangle number.

E1 Instead of using dots we can use unit squares:

The 10th triangle number will be the number of unit squares in this diagram. In other words, it is the **area** of the diagram.

The area can be split up into a triangle (shaded) and some extra 'half-squares'.

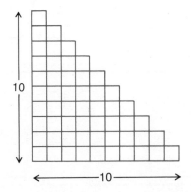

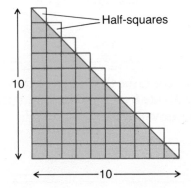

Half-squares

(a) What is the area of the shaded triangle?
(b) How many extra half-squares are there? What is their total area?
(c) What is the total area of the diagram?

60

E2 Check your answer to question E1 by doing $1+2+3+4+\ldots$ up to 10.

E3 Imagine the 'unit squares' diagram for the 12th triangle number. Imagine it split up into a shaded triangle and some extra half-squares.

(a) What is the area of the shaded triangle?

(b) How many extra half-squares are there? What is their total area?

(c) What is the total area of the diagram?

(d) Check that $1+2+3+4+\ldots$ up to 12 gives the same answer.

E4 Imagine the diagram for the 50th triangle number, and calculate the 50th triangle number in a similar way.

The method used in questions E1 to E4 can be used to give a formula for working out the nth triangle number.

The next question shows how this can be done.

E5 Imagine the 'unit squares' diagram for the nth triangle number.

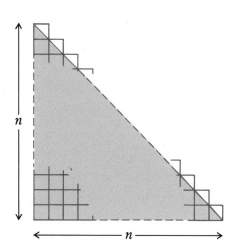

(a) Write an expression for the area of the shaded triangle.

(b) How many extra half-squares are there? Write an expression for their total area.

(c) Write an expression for the total area of the diagram.

E6 Show that the formula you found in question E5 can also be written like this:

$$n\text{th triangle number} = \frac{n(n+1)}{2}$$

*E7 The diagram for the nth triangle number can be fitted against a copy of itself like this.

Use this to explain how to get the formula given in question E6.

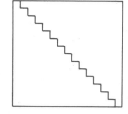

8 Types of proportionality

A Direct and inverse proportionality

Direct proprotionality

When a motorist buys petrol, the cost of the petrol is directly proportional to the quantity.
Doubling the quantity doubles the cost. Trebling the quantity trebles the cost and so on.

The symbol for 'is proportional to' is $\propto$. So we can write

Cost of petrol $\propto$ quantity

The graph of (quantity, cost) is a straight line going through $(0, 0)$.

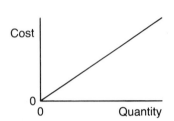

Inverse proportionality

For an example of inverse proportionality, think of a journey, and of the relationship between speed and journey time.

Suppose that at a speed of 40 m.p.h. the journey time would be 6 hours.

Doubling the speed halves the journey time to 3 hours.
If the speed is multiplied by 3, the journey time is divided by 3, and so on.

Dividing by 3 is the same as multiplying by the **reciprocal** of 3, or $\frac{1}{3}$.

So we can also say: if we multiply the speed by a number n, then the journey time is multiplied by $\frac{1}{n}$.

'The journey time is inversely proportional to the speed' is written using the symbol $\propto$ like this:

Journey time $\propto \dfrac{1}{\text{speed}}$

If the speed is multiplied by, say, 1·6 then the journey time is multiplied by $\frac{1}{1\cdot6}$, or 0·625.

A1 Ohm's law states that if a voltage V volts is applied across the terminals of an electrical component, and if I amps is the current flowing in the component, then $I \propto V$.

With a certain component it is found that when $V = 15$ then $I = 2 \cdot 5$.

Calculate I when V is   (a) 60   (b) 6   (c) 0·6   (d) 25

A2 If w m is the wavelength of a sound wave and f hertz is the frequency of the wave, then $w \propto \dfrac{1}{f}$.

A sound wave with frequency 300 hertz has a wavelength of 1·1 m. Calculate the wavelength of a sound wave with frequency

(a) 3000 hertz   (b) 30 hertz   (c) 150 hertz   (d) 660 hertz

A3 P and Q are two variables, and $Q \propto P$.

Find the multipliers and the missing value in this table.

P	14·9	8·3
Q	5·2	...

A4 R and S are two variables and $S \propto \dfrac{1}{R}$.

Find the multipliers and the missing value in this table.

R	9·5	6·6
S	4·8	...

A5 If $Y \propto \dfrac{1}{X}$ and X is multiplied by $\frac{5}{8}$, what is Y multiplied by?

A6 $B \propto A$, and $B = 20 \cdot 3$ when $A = 18 \cdot 4$. Calculate B when $A = 31 \cdot 2$.

A7 $Y \propto \dfrac{1}{X}$, and $Y = 46 \cdot 3$ when $X = 4 \cdot 2$. Calculate Y when $X = 17 \cdot 8$.

*A8 The time for a journey is inversely proportional to the speed. Calculate the percentage increase or decrease in the journey time when the speed is

(a) increased by 50%   (b) decreased by 50%

(c) increased by 20%   (d) decreased by 20%

B Other types of proportionality

A manufacturer makes square tiles, of different sizes.

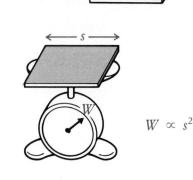

They are all made from the same material and have the same thickness, so the **weight** of a tile is proportional to its **area**.

> **Weight ∝ Area**

If s stands for the length of the side of a tile, the area of the tile is s^2.

So we can say that the weight, W, is proportional to s^2, which we write

> $W \propto s^2$.

$W \propto s^2$

For example, suppose we have two tiles, of sides 10 cm and 30 cm, and that the smaller tile weighs 250 g.

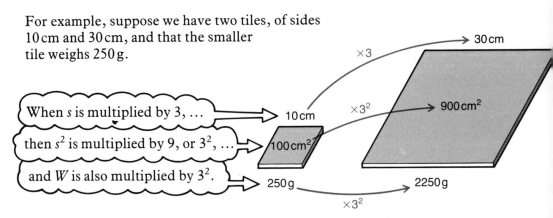

When s is multiplied by 3, ...

then s^2 is multiplied by 9, or 3^2, ...

and W is also multiplied by 3^2.

When you multiply s by a number, then W is multiplied by the **square** of that number.

B1 If A cm^2 is the area of a TV screen and d cm is the length of its diagonal, then $A \propto d^2$.

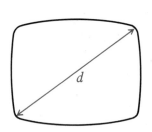

(a) If you multiply d by 4, what do you multiply A by?

(b) A TV screen with a diagonal of 15 cm has an area of 110 cm^2. What is the area of a screen with diagonal 60 cm?

(c) Copy and complete this table to find the area of a screen with diagonal 21 cm.

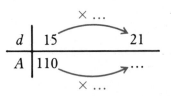

	× ...	
d	15	21
A	110	...
	× ...	

B2 The wind resistance on a train is proportional to the square of the train's speed.

    (a) If the speed is doubled, what happens to the wind resistance?

    (b) What happens to the resistance when the speed is multiplied by 1·5?

B3 If a ball is thrown upwards with speed u m/s and rises to a height of h m, then $h \propto u^2$.

    Given that h is 90 when u is 42, calculate h when u is 65. (You may find it helpful to use a table similar to the one in question B1.)

B4 The surface area of a sphere is proportional to the square of its diameter.

    (a) The diameter of Mars is approximately twice the diameter of the moon. The surface area of the moon is approximately $3·8 \times 10^7$ km^2. Calculate the surface area of Mars, approximately.

    (b) The diameter of Saturn is approximately 10 times that of Venus. The surface area of Venus is approximately $2·8 \times 10^{12}$ km^2. Calculate the surface area of Saturn, approximately.

B5 When an object is dropped, the distance d metres which it falls in t seconds is proportional to t^2.

    If $d = 78·4$ when $t = 4·0$, calculate d when $t = 7·0$.

Another type of proportionality is where one variable is proportional to the **cube** of another.

The volume of a sphere is proportional to the cube of the diameter.

If you multiply the diameter by a number, the volume is multiplied by the cube of the number.

The diameter of Saturn is 10 times that of Venus.

The volume of Saturn is 10^3, or 1000, times that of Venus.

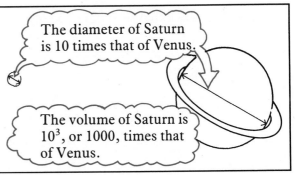

B6 The diameter of a spherical balloon is increased from 20 cm to 30 cm. What is the volume of the balloon multiplied by?

B7 If P is the power output of a windmill and v is the speed of the wind, then $P \propto v^3$.

    (a) What happens to P if v is multiplied by 3?

    (b) What is P multiplied by when v increases from 40 m.p.h. to 50 m.p.h.?

Yet another type of proportionality is where one variable is proportional to the **square root** of another.

The time of swing of a pendulum is proportional to the square root of its length.

If T stands for the time of swing and l for the length, then $T \propto \sqrt{l}$.

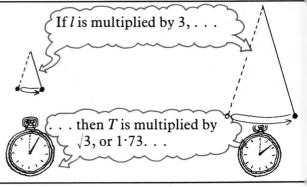

If l is multiplied by 3, . . .

. . . then T is multiplied by $\sqrt{3}$, or 1·73. . .

B8 What happens to T when l is multiplied by

(a) 2   (b) 4   (c) 5   (d) 10   (e) 20

B9 A ball rolls down a slope. If v m/s is the speed of the ball after travelling a distance of d m down the slope, then $v \propto \sqrt{d}$.

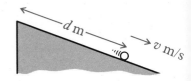

(a) What is v multiplied by when d increases from 2 m to 5 m?

(b) If $v = 4 \cdot 5$ when $d = 5$, what is v when $d = 8$?

The 'inverse square law'

A satellite (or a spacecraft) is pulled towards the Earth by the force of gravity. The strength of this force depends on the distance of the satellite from the Earth. If F is the force and d is the distance, measured from the Earth's centre,

then it is known that $F \propto \dfrac{1}{d^2}$. (This is sometimes called an 'inverse square law'.)

So, for example, if d is multiplied by 3, then F is multiplied by $\dfrac{1}{3^2}$ or $\dfrac{1}{9}$.

B10 An object on the Earth's surface is about 6400 km from the Earth's centre If this distance is doubled, so that the object is now 12 800 km from

the centre, the force of gravity is multiplied by $\dfrac{1}{2^2}$. That means

the force of gravity is $\dfrac{1}{4}$ of what it is at the Earth's surface.

What can you say about the force of gravity 64 000 km from the centre?

⋆**B11** If $Y \propto X^2$, what is the percentage change in Y when X is

(a) increased by 25%   (b) decreased by 25%

⋆**B12** If $Y \propto \dfrac{1}{X^2}$, what is the percentage change in Y when X is

(a) increased by 30%   (b) decreased by 30%

C Searching for proportionality

Marcus was doing some experiments to find the greatest load
which various thicknesses of rope would hold without breaking.

These were the results he got.

Diameter of rope, in mm	5	8	12	18	28	35
Maximum load, in kg	3·8	9·6	21·8	48·5	117·3	185·0

Marcus suspected that the maximum load is proportional to the
square of the diameter, and he wanted to find out if this is true.

So he made a new table showing (diameter)² and load.

(Diameter)²	25	64	144	324	784	1225
Maximum load	3·8	9·6	21·8	48·5	117·3	185·0

C1   Draw a graph with (diameter)² across
and load up. Use the scales shown here.
Plot the six points from the table.

(a) Is it true that
maximum load $\propto$ (diameter)²?

(b) If you double the diameter of
the rope, what effect does this have
on the maximum load?

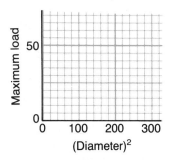

C2   Kate was doing an experiment with a ball bearing rolling down
a sloping groove. She let the ball go at the top of the groove and then
measured how far it had rolled at various different times.

Here are her results.

Time in seconds	0	4	7	10	15
Distance in cm	0	30	92	188	422

(a) Kate thought that the distance should be proportional to the time.
Draw a graph with **time** across and **distance** up. Is the distance
proportional to the time?

(b) Draw another graph with (**time**)² across and **distance** up. Is the
distance proportional to the square of the time?

C3   This table shows the frequency, f Hz, of the note
produced by a string when it is stretched by a
weight, w kg, hanging on one end.

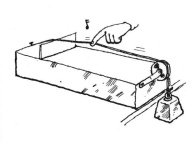

w	1·5	2·4	3·3	5·6	7·5
f	120	152	178	232	268

Find out by drawing graphs which of these is
true: $f \propto w$ $f \propto w^2$ $f \propto w^3$ $f \propto \sqrt{w}$

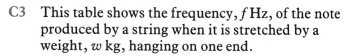
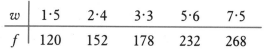

9 Manipulating formulas

A Substitution from one formula into another (1)

Four quantities which are of great importance to electricians are
    P, the power consumed in an appliance (measured in watts),
    V, the voltage across the appliance (measured in volts),
    I, the current through the appliance (measured in amps),
    R, the resistance of the appliance (measured in ohms).

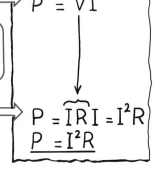

These quantities are connected by two formulas: (1) $P = VI$
                                                     (2) $V = IR$

Formula (1) connects P with V and I.
Formula (2) connects V with I and R.

Suppose an electrician is not interested in V (perhaps she does not know what the value of V is). She wants a formula for P in terms of I and R, not mentioning V. She can get it like this:

1 She wants a formula for P. She starts with the formula which begins $P = ...$ This is formula (1).

$P = VI$

2 She wants to eliminate V from this formula.
She uses the other formula to get an expression for V.
From formula (2) she knows that V is equal to IR.

3 She substitutes IR for V in formula (1).

The final formula does not mention V.

$P = \overparen{IRI} = I^2R$
$\underline{P = I^2R}$

A1 You are given the two formulas (1) $F = ma$
                                           (2) $W = Fs$

      Find a formula for W in terms of a, m and s.

A2 You are given the two formulas (1) $m = \dfrac{r}{s}$

                                           (2) $k = mr$

      Find a formula for k in terms of r and s.

A3 You are given the two formulas (1) $q = \dfrac{a}{c}$

                                           (2) $p = c^2q$

      Find a formula for p in terms of a and c.

Sometimes we have to insert **brackets** when we substitute into a formula.

For example, if $q = a - bc$ and $c = x - y$, we can replace c in the first formula by $x - y$. When we do this we put brackets round $x - y$.

$$q = a - bc = a - b(x - y)$$

Afterwards we can multiply out the brackets, following the usual rules.

$$q = a - bx + by$$

A4 Given that $y = 3 + 4x$ and $x = a - 2b$, find a formula for y in terms of a and b.

A5 If $z = 3x - 2y$ and $x = a + b$ and $y = a - b$, find a formula for z in terms of a and b.

A6 If $r = 4p - q$ and $p = x - 2y$ and $q = x - 5y$, find a formula for r in terms of x and y.

A7 If $z = 2a + 7b$ and $a = n + 1$ and $b = 4 - 3n$, find a formula for z in terms of n.

A8 If $q = pr$ and $p = x + 5$ and $r = y + 2$, find a formula for q in terms of x and y. Multiply out the brackets.

A9 If $t = su$ and $s = a - 3$ and $u = a + 4$, find a formula for t in terms of a. Multiply out the brackets.

A10 If $c = 2ab$ and $a = x + 5$ and $b = x - 1$, find a formula for c in terms of x. Multiply out the brackets.

Worked example

If $c = ab^2$ and $b = 3k$, find a formula for c in terms of a and k.

Replace b in the first formula by $3k$. So b^2 becomes $(3k)^2$, which is $3k \times 3k$ or $9k^2$.

So $c = ab^2 = a \times 9k^2 = 9ak^2$.

A11 If $D = 2a^2$ and $a = 5b$, find a formula for D in terms of b.

A12 If $S = kp^2$ and $p = 4t$, find a formula for S in terms of k and t.

A13 If $H = 5x^2$ and $x = an$, find a formula for H in terms of a and n.

A14 If $I = md^2$ and $d = \dfrac{r}{2m}$, find a formula for I in terms

of m and r and simplify it as far as possible.

B Substitution (2)

If we are given the two formulas (1) $P = VI$ and (2) $V = IR$, we can get a formula for P in terms of V and R, eliminating I.

1 We want a formula for P. So we start with formula (1) because it begins $P = \ldots$

2 We want to eliminate I. We use the other formula to get an expression for I.

To do this we have to do some extra work, re-arranging formula (2) to make I its subject.

3 Now we substitute for I in formula (1).

The final formula does not mention I.

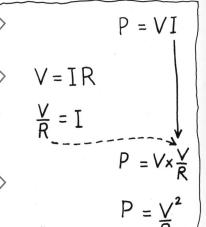

$$P = VI$$

$$V = IR$$

$$\frac{V}{R} = I$$

$$P = V \times \frac{V}{R}$$

$$P = \frac{V^2}{R}$$

B1 You are given the two formulas   (1) $k = 4a$
                                             (2) $m = ab$

Find a formula for k in terms of m and b.
(Start with the formula which begins $k = \ldots$ You want to eliminate a. Use the other formula to get an expresion for a.)

B2 You are given the two formulas   (1) $r = mk$
                                             (2) $b = \dfrac{k}{c}$

Find a formula for r in terms of m, b and c.

B3 You are given the two formulas   (1) $g = \dfrac{r}{s}$
                                             (2) $t = as$

Find a formula for t in terms of a, r and g.

B4 You are given the two formulas   (1) $v = nw$ (2) $T = \dfrac{2\pi}{n}$

Find a formula for v in terms of T, w and π.

B5 You are given the formulas   (1) $C = 2\pi r$ (2) $A = \pi r^2$

Find a formula for A in terms of C and r, eliminating π.

Worked example

From the formulas   (1) $v = at$
                           (2) $s = \frac{1}{2}at^2$

find a formula for s in terms of a and v only.

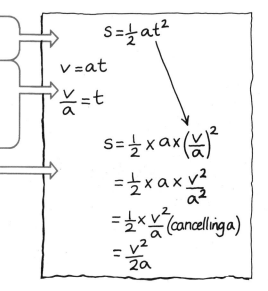

1 We want a formula for s. Formula (2) begins $s = \ldots$, so we start with that.

2 We want s in terms of a and v. So we must eliminate t.

Re-arrange formula (1) to make t its subject.

3 Substitute for t in formula (2). Notice the **brackets**.

$$s = \frac{1}{2}at^2$$

$$v = at$$

$$\frac{v}{a} = t$$

$$s = \frac{1}{2} \times a \times \left(\frac{v}{a}\right)^2$$

$$= \frac{1}{2} \times a \times \frac{v^2}{a^2}$$

$$= \frac{1}{2} \times \frac{v^2}{a} \text{ (cancelling } a)$$

$$= \frac{v^2}{2a}$$

B6   From the formulas   (1) $d = 2r$ (2) $A = \pi r^2$
find a formula for A in terms of π and d.

B7   From the formulas   (1) $v = at$ (2) $s = \frac{1}{2}at^2$
find a formula for s in terms of v and t.

B8   From the formulas   (1) $v = wr$ (2) $a = w^2r$
find a formula for a in terms of v and w.

B9   From the formulas   (1) $v = wr$ (2) $a = w^2r$
find a formula for a in terms of v and r.

B10   From the formulas $p = mv$ and $T = \frac{1}{2}mv^2$,
find a formula for T in terms of p and v.

B11   From the formulas $p = mv$ and $T = \frac{1}{2}mv^2$,
find a formula for T in terms of m and p.

B12   From the formulas $C = 2\pi r$ and $A = \pi r^2$,
find a formula for A in terms of π and C.

B13   From the formulas $k = \dfrac{A}{u}$ and $L = \dfrac{u^2}{m}$,

find a formula for L in terms of A, k and m.

The next worked example involves dividing by a fraction.

Worked example

If $r = \dfrac{s}{t}$ and $t = \dfrac{m}{a}$, find a formula for r in terms of s, m and a.

Replace t in the first formula by $\dfrac{m}{a}$.

So $r = \dfrac{s}{t} = \dfrac{s}{\left(\dfrac{m}{a}\right)} = s \times \dfrac{a}{m}$ (from the rule for dividing by a fraction).

So $r = \dfrac{sa}{m}$.

B14 If $b = \dfrac{a}{2}$ and $c = \dfrac{d}{a}$, find a formula for c in terms of b and d.

B15 If $a = \dfrac{v^2}{r}$ and $r = \dfrac{d}{2}$, find a in terms of d and v.

B16 If $K = \dfrac{P}{2r}$ and $r = \dfrac{h}{a}$, find K in terms of P, h and a.

Worked example

If $D = \dfrac{M}{V}$ and $PV = K$, find a formula for D in terms of K, M and P.

We need to eliminate V from the formula for D.

From the second formula $PV = K$, we get $V = \dfrac{K}{P}$.

So we have to substitute $\dfrac{K}{P}$ for V in the first formula.

So $D = \dfrac{M}{\left(\dfrac{K}{P}\right)} = M \times \dfrac{P}{K} = \dfrac{MP}{K}$.

Another method uses the fact that the value of a fraction is unchanged when its top and bottom are multiplied by the same number.

$$D = \frac{M}{V} = \frac{MP}{VP} \text{ (multiplying top and bottom by } P) = \frac{MP}{K}.$$

B17 If $T = \dfrac{2\pi}{n}$ and $v = nw$, find T in terms of π, v and w.

B18 If $r = \dfrac{s^2}{t}$ and $t = \dfrac{u}{s}$, find r in terms of s and u.

B19 If $p = \dfrac{a}{k^2}$ and $y = kx$, find p in terms of a, x and y.

C Re-arranging a formula containing a square root

If we start with a number (say 25), take its square root (5) and then square this square root (5^2), we obviously get back to our starting number.

Squaring **undoes** the effect of taking the square root. We use this fact to remove square roots from formulas, as in the next example.

Worked example

Re-arrange the formula $a = b\sqrt{(rs)}$ to make r the subject.

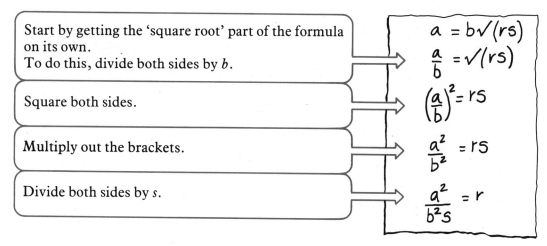

Start by getting the 'square root' part of the formula on its own. To do this, divide both sides by b.	$a = b\sqrt{(rs)}$ $\dfrac{a}{b} = \sqrt{(rs)}$
Square both sides.	$\left(\dfrac{a}{b}\right)^2 = rs$
Multiply out the brackets.	$\dfrac{a^2}{b^2} = rs$
Divide both sides by s.	$\dfrac{a^2}{b^2 s} = r$

C1 The time of one complete swing of a simple pendulum is given approximately by the formula $T = 2\sqrt{l}$, where T is the time in seconds and l is the length of the pendulum in metres.

(a) Make l the subject of the formula.
(b) Calculate l when T is 15.

C2 When an object is thrown vertically upwards, in order to reach a height h metres it must be thrown with a speed of u m/s, where u is given approximately by the formula $u = \sqrt{(20h)}$.

Make h the subject of this formula.

C3 Make m the subject of the formula   (a) $t = \dfrac{\sqrt{m}}{a}$ (b) $t = \sqrt{\left(\dfrac{m}{a}\right)}$

C4 Make s the subject of the formula $v = \sqrt{(2gs)}$.

C5 Make q the subject of the formula $k = 3\sqrt{\left(\dfrac{q}{s}\right)}$.

C6 (a) Make l the subject of the formula $T = 2\pi\sqrt{\left(\dfrac{l}{g}\right)}$.

(b) Make g the subject of the same formula.

73

GRID REFERENCES

This is part of an **Ordnance Survey** map.

The scale of this map is 2 cm to 1 km.

The map is also called a 1 : 50 000 ('one to fifty thousand') map, because 1 cm represents 50 000 cm, which is 0·5 km.

The map is covered by a grid of squares, each representing a square 1 km by 1 km. The numbers along the edges of the map can be used to name the squares.

Look at the coloured square. Look at its **bottom left-hand corner**. Its 'coordinates' are 12 (across) and 16 (up).
We say the **grid reference** of this square is 1216 ('one two one six').

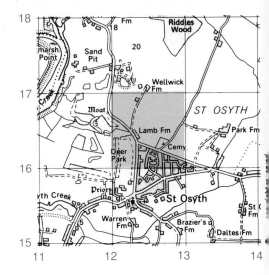

Always use the bottom left-hand corner for finding the grid reference of a square.

1 What is the grid reference of the square containing
(a) Daltes Farm   (b) Wellwick Farm   (c) Park Farm

We can also give grid references for points on the map.

Find St Osyth church (marked ♠) in square 1215.

The sides of the square can be divided into tenths.
The church is 12·3 across and 15·6 up.

We leave out the decimal points, and write the grid reference with six figures, like this: 123156

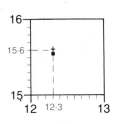

You have to estimate the tenths from the map.

2 Write down the six-figure grid reference for
(a) Daltes Farm   (b) Wellwick Farm   (c) Park Farm

3 What is situated at   (a) 123165   (b) 129152   (c) 127163

4 **Calculate** the distance between the points with grid references 113157 and 135174, showing your method clearly.

5 Calculate the distance between 114178 and 130154.

10 Probability

A Spinnners

These diagrams show a kind of spinner.

The circle is divided into coloured parts, or **sectors**. The arrow is spun, and when it stops it will be in one of the sectors.

On this spinner there are three sectors of equal size, so the probability that the arrow stops in, say, the red sector is $\frac{1}{3}$.

(We ignore the possibility that the arrow stops **exactly** on the boundary line between two sectors. If this should happen, the arrow can be spun again.)

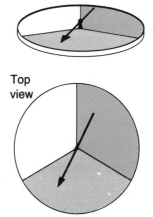

Top view

A1 Write down the probability of getting 'red' with each of these spinners.

(a) 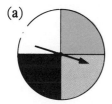 (b) 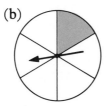 (c) 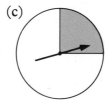 (d)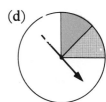

Spinners can be used to represent other situations where the outcome is a matter of chance. Here are some examples.

A throw of an ordinary dice can be represented like this.

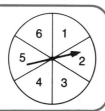

A throw of an ordinary coin can be represented like this.

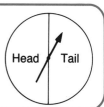

Head Tail

This spinner represents a throw of a drawing-pin if the probability of landing 'point up' is $\frac{3}{4}$.

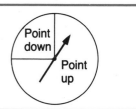

Point down

Point up

B Independent events

Suppose we have two spinners, 1 and 2, as shown here.

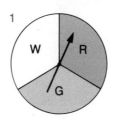
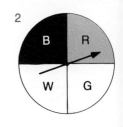

We spin both of them.

The two spinners do not affect each other. The result on spinner 2 is **independent** of the result on spinner 1.

The possible outcomes of the pair of spins can be shown in a table like this.

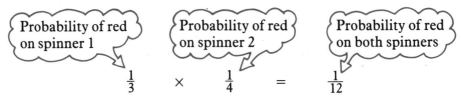

Spinner 2

	R	G	W	B
R	RR	RG	RW	RB
G	GR	GG	GW	GB
W	WR	WG	WW	WB

Spinner 1

This means 'red on spinner 1 and black on spinner 2'.

There are 12 equally likely outcomes for the pair of spins. So the probability of each outcome is $\frac{1}{12}$.

So, for example, the probability of getting RR (red, red) is $\frac{1}{12}$.

Notice that you can get this probability by **multiplying** the probability of red on spinner 1 ($\frac{1}{3}$) by the probability of red on spinner 2 ($\frac{1}{4}$).

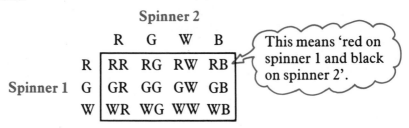

Probability of red on spinner 1

Probability of red on spinner 2

Probability of red on both spinners

$$\frac{1}{3} \quad \times \quad \frac{1}{4} \quad = \quad \frac{1}{12}$$

This illustrates a general rule about **independent** events.

> If two events are **independent**, the probability that they **both** happen is found by multiplying their probabilities together.

B1 These two spinners are spun.

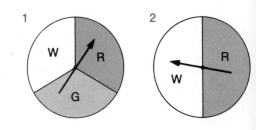

(a) Make a table showing all the equally likely outcomes of the pair of spins.

(b) What is the probability that both spins give red?

(c) Check that the rule given above is true here.

B2 Two coins are thrown.
What is the probability that both of them give heads?

B3 Two dice are thrown.
Calculate the probability that both of them give sixes.

These two spinners have numbers on them as well as colours.

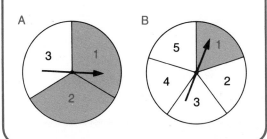

The equally likely outcomes for a pair of spins are shown in this table.

Spinner B

		1	2	3	4	5
Spinner A	1	1,1	1,2	1,3	1,4	1,5
	2	2,1	2,2	2,3	2,4	2,5
	3	3,1	3,2	3,3	3,4	3,5

There are 15 equally likely outcomes in the table.
In 2 of them, spinner A gives red and spinner B gives red.
So the probability that A and B **both** give red is $\frac{2}{15}$.

This probability can be found by **multiplying**.

$$\frac{2}{3} \quad \times \quad \frac{1}{5} \quad = \quad \frac{2}{15}$$

Red on A   Red on B   Red on both

B4 (a) In how many of the 15 outcomes in the table above does spinner A give red and spinner B white?

(b) Write down the probability of getting 'red on A and white on B'.

(c) Check that the multiplication rule works here.

(d) Check that the rule also works for the probability of 'white on A and red on B'.

(e) Check that the rule works for 'white on A and white on B'.

B5 These two spinners are spun.

(a) Write down the probability of
   (i) red on spinner A
   (ii) white on spinner A
   (iii) red on spinner B
   (iv) white on spinner B

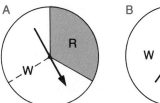
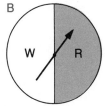

(b) Use the multiplication rule to work out the probability of
   (i) red on A and red on B   (ii) red on A and white on B
   (iii) white on A and red on B   (iv) white on A and white on B

c Tree diagrams

The outcomes of a spin of this spinner

can be shown in a very simple **tree diagram**. We write the probability of each outcome on its branch.

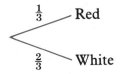

The outcomes of two spins can be shown in a larger tree diagram.
A red on the first spin can be followed by a red or a white.
A white on the first spin can be followed by a red or a white.

The probabilities are the same for the second spin, because the two spins are independent. (The result of the first does not affect the second.)

We can calculate the probability of each outcome by multiplying the fractions along each route through the diagram.

1st spin	2nd spin	Outcome	Probability
$\frac{1}{3}$ Red	$\frac{1}{3}$ Red	Red, Red	$\frac{1}{3} \times \frac{1}{3} = \frac{1}{9}$
	$\frac{2}{3}$ White	Red, White	$\frac{1}{3} \times \frac{2}{3} = \frac{2}{9}$
$\frac{2}{3}$ White	$\frac{1}{3}$ Red	White, Red	$\frac{2}{3} \times \frac{1}{3} = \frac{2}{9}$
	$\frac{2}{3}$ White	White, White	$\frac{2}{3} \times \frac{2}{3} = \frac{4}{9}$

C1 What do the four probabilities at the right of the diagram add up to? Is this what you would expect?

C2 Draw a similar tree diagram for two spins of this spinner.
Calculate the probabilities of the four outcomes, as in the table above.

Check that the probabilities add up to 1.

C3 Repeat question C2 for two spins of this spinner.

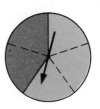

C4 A printer is printing the pages of a book. Each page has black print and red print on it, and it goes through two separate printing machines, one for each colour.

Unfortunately, both machines are unreliable. The black machine fails to print sometimes and lets a blank sheet through. The probability that this happens is $\frac{1}{5}$.

The red machine is even more unreliable. The probability that it fails to print is $\frac{1}{4}$. The two machines work independently of each other.

(a) Copy and complete this tree diagram. It will show the different outcomes which can happen when a sheet goes through both machines. Write the probabilities on the branches.

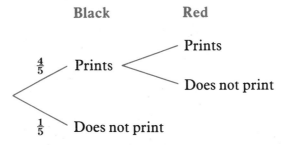

(b) Calculate the probability that a sheet is printed
    (i) black and red   (ii) black but not red
  (iii) red but not black   (iv) neither colour

C5 The printer in question C4 now has to print three colours, black, red and blue. He uses the same machines as before for the black and the red. His blue printing machine is also unreliable. The probability that it fails to print is $\frac{1}{10}$.

(a) Draw a tree diagram to show the outcomes of all three machines. It will look something like this.

(b) Calculate the probability that a sheet is printed
    (i) black and red but not blue   (ii) red and blue but not black

D Adding probabilities

A sheet of paper goes through two unreliable printing machines.
The first machine prints in black. The probability that it fails to
print is $\frac{1}{4}$.
The second machine prints in red. The probability that it fails to
print is $\frac{1}{6}$.

This tree diagram shows all the outcomes.

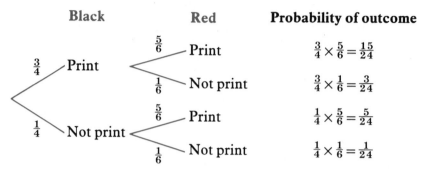

Suppose we want to know the probability that **just one colour** is printed
(either black or red).
There are two different ways for this to happen: black prints but not red,
red prints but not black.

From the tree diagram, the probability of 'black but not red' is $\frac{3}{4} \times \frac{1}{6} = \frac{3}{24}$.

The probability of 'red but not black' is $\frac{1}{4} \times \frac{5}{6} = \frac{5}{24}$.

So the total probability that just one colour is printed is $\frac{3}{24} + \frac{5}{24} = \frac{8}{24}$.

We can add this information to the diagram.

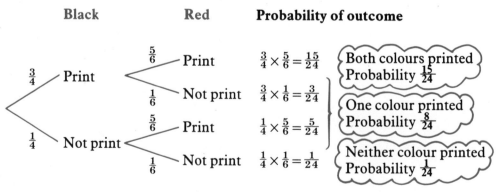

Notice that none of the fractions have been simplified. They are
easier to add together if they are not simplified.

> **D1** Look back at the tree diagram you drew for question C4.
> Calculate the probability that just one colour is printed.

D2 This tree diagram shows two throws of a dice.
Copy the diagram and write the probabilities of 'six' and
'not six' on the branches.

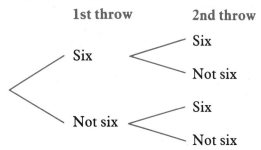

1st throw   2nd throw

Six   Six
      Not six

Not six   Six
      Not six

Calculate the probability of getting
(a) two sixes   (b) one six   (c) no sixes

D3 The spinner on the left is spun twice.

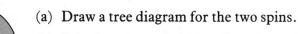

(a) Draw a tree diagram for the two spins.

(b) Calculate the probability of getting red
     (i) once   (ii) twice   (iii) not at all

(c) Which of these three is most likely to happen?

D4 Do the same as in question D3 for this spinner.

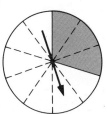

D5 The tree diagrams on the opposite page are for a sheet
of paper going through two printing machines.

The diagram below is for **two** sheets of paper going through
one printing machine. The machine is unreliable: the
probability that it prints is $\frac{4}{5}$.

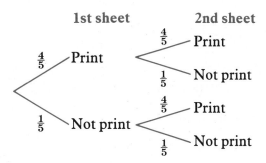

1st sheet   2nd sheet

$\frac{4}{5}$ Print
    $\frac{4}{5}$ Print
    $\frac{1}{5}$ Not print

$\frac{1}{5}$ Not print
    $\frac{4}{5}$ Print
    $\frac{1}{5}$ Not print

Calculate the probability that

(a) both sheets are printed   (b) only one sheet is printed
(c) neither sheet is printed

E Adding fractions

The top number of a fraction is called its **numerator**, and the bottom number its **denominator**.

So far, we have only needed to add fractions whose denominators are the same. For example, $\frac{3}{24} + \frac{5}{24} = \frac{8}{24}$.

In the section after this, you will need to add fractions with different denominators, for example, $\frac{3}{4} + \frac{1}{6}$.

You can do it in this way.

1 Think of fractions which are equal to $\frac{3}{4}$.

$$\frac{3}{4} = \frac{6}{8} = \frac{9}{12} = \frac{12}{16} = \ldots$$

2 Think of fractions which are equal to $\frac{1}{6}$.

$$\frac{1}{6} = \frac{2}{12} = \frac{3}{18} = \frac{4}{24} = \ldots$$

3 Choose a fraction from each list with the same denominator.

$$\frac{9}{12}, \frac{2}{12}$$

4 $\frac{3}{4} + \frac{1}{6}$

$$= \frac{9}{12} + \frac{2}{12} = \frac{11}{12}$$

E1 Work these out.

(a) $\frac{1}{2} + \frac{1}{3}$ (b) $\frac{1}{2} + \frac{1}{6}$ (c) $\frac{3}{4} + \frac{1}{6}$ (d) $\frac{3}{4} + \frac{1}{5}$

(e) $\frac{2}{3} + \frac{1}{4}$ (f) $\frac{2}{5} + \frac{3}{8}$ (g) $\frac{5}{12} + \frac{3}{8}$ (h) $\frac{2}{5} + \frac{1}{3}$

E2 Work these out.

(a) $\frac{2}{3} - \frac{1}{2}$ (b) $\frac{3}{5} - \frac{1}{4}$ (c) $\frac{5}{8} - \frac{1}{3}$ (d) $\frac{3}{4} - \frac{2}{3}$

(e) $\frac{5}{6} - \frac{3}{4}$ (f) $\frac{3}{8} - \frac{1}{6}$ (g) $\frac{3}{4} - \frac{3}{5}$ (h) $\frac{2}{5} - \frac{1}{4}$

E3 Let h stand for $\frac{1}{2}$, t for $\frac{1}{3}$, q for $\frac{1}{4}$ and f for $\frac{1}{5}$.

You can get other fractions by adding together multiples of h, t, q and f. For example, $2t + f = \frac{2}{3} + \frac{1}{5} = \frac{10}{15} + \frac{3}{15} = \frac{13}{15}$.

(a) Work these out.

   (i) $h + f$ (ii) $h + 2f$ (iii) $q + 3f$ (iv) $h + q + f$

(b) Find as many different combinations of h, t, q and f as you can which give fractions less than 1. For example, $2t + f$ is $\frac{13}{15}$, so $2t + f$ is one possible combination.

F Dependent events

Sonya starts at the point marked A on this map, and walks towards B.

When she gets to B she **tosses a coin**. If she gets a head, she turns left. If she gets a tail, she turns right.

If she gets to C, she **tosses the coin** again. As before, a head means she turns left and a tail right.

If she gets to D, she **throws a dice**. If she gets a six, she turns left; if not, she turns right.

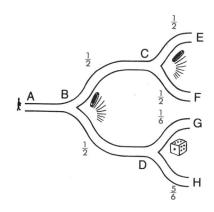

In this example, the probability that Sonya's second turn is to the left **does** depend on which way she turned before.
If she turns left the first time, the probability of turning left the second time is $\frac{1}{2}$.
If she turns right the first time, the probability of turning left the second time is $\frac{1}{6}$.

The probabilities marked on the map (which is itself a tree diagram) are the probabilities of turning left or right at each place **if she gets there**.

As before, we can multiply along each route.
The probability that Sonya follows the route ABCE is $\frac{1}{2} \times \frac{1}{2} = \frac{1}{4}$.

F1 What is the probability that Sonya follows the route

(a) ABCF (b) ABDG (c) ABDH

F2 Suppose F and G are not two different places, but the same place. What is the probability that Sonya gets to this place? (She can get there by two different routes. Add up the probabilities of these two routes.)

F3 Scott starts at P on this map. The probability that he turns left or right at each junction is marked on the map.

(a) Calculate the probability that he gets to (i) Q (ii) R (iii) S

(b) Which of the three places is he least likely to get to?

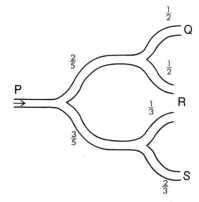

F4 A cat has three favourite sleeping places: under the stairs, on top of the cupboard, and behind the boiler.
Call these three places S (stairs), C (cupboard) and B (boiler).

Each night the cat chooses one of its sleeping places. The probability that it chooses the same place as the previous night is $\frac{1}{4}$. The probabilities of choosing each of the other places are equal.

Last night the cat slept under the stairs.

(a) What is the probability that tonight the cat will sleep

    (i) under the stairs   (ii) on top of the cupboard
  (iii) behind the boiler

(b) Draw a tree diagram like this with the three probabilities marked on it. Extend the diagram to show what can happen tomorrow night.

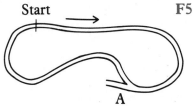

Last night   **Tonight**   **Tomorrow night**

(c) Calculate the probability that in the three nights (last night, tonight, tomorrow night) the cat sleeps under the stairs

    (i) three times   (ii) twice only   (iii) once only

Start

F5 A car goes round this track. When it gets to the point A, it may go off the track. The probability that this happens is $\frac{1}{10}$.

If it goes off the track, it stays off. Otherwise it goes round again. Each time it approaches A there is a $\frac{1}{10}$ chance that it will go off the track.

The tree diagram below shows what can happen the first and second times the car goes round the track.

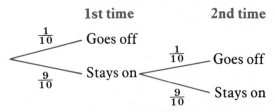

1st time   **2nd time**

(a) Copy the tree diagram and continue it to show the 3rd and 4th times.

(b) Calculate the probability that the car is still on the track after going round four times.

Taking counters from a bag

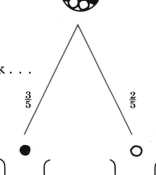

A bag contains 5 counters.
3 are black and 2 white.

Someone takes out two
counters at random.

The first counter can be black . . .   . . . or white.

The probability that the $\frac{3}{5}$ $\frac{2}{5}$ The probability that the
first counter is black is $\frac{3}{5}$.   first counter is white is $\frac{2}{5}$.

If the first one taken out is   ●   ○   If the first one taken out is
black, that leaves 2 black   white, that leaves 3 black
and 2 white in the bag.   and 1 white in the bag.

If the first one taken out is $\frac{2}{4}$ $\frac{2}{4}$ $\frac{3}{4}$ $\frac{1}{4}$ **If the first one taken out is**
black, the probabilities for   **white**, the probabilities for
the second counter are as   the second counter are as
shown here.   shown here.

● ○   ● ○

F6   Use the tree diagram above to calculate the probability
of getting

(a) two black counters
(b) one counter of each colour
(c) two white counters

F7   Draw a similar tree diagram for taking two counters
from a bag containing 3 black counters and 5 white
counters.

Calculate the probabilities asked for in question F6.

F8   Do the same as in question F7 for a bag containing
7 black counters and 3 white counters.

F9   In my pocket I have 4 twopence pieces, 3 fivepence pieces and
2 twenty-pence pieces.

I put my hand in my pocket and take out two coins at random.
Calculate the probability that

(a) they are both fivepence pieces

(b) they are both the same type of coin

85

11 Sequences (2)

A Suffix notation

When you are referring to a particular sequence, it is often useful
to have a symbol for it. Letters are used for sequences, and a small
number (or letter) called a **suffix** is written below and to the right of
the sequence letter to show the position of a term in the sequence.

For example, suppose the letter a is used for this sequence.

Position	1	2	3	4	5	. . .
Term	3	8	13	18	23	. . .

Then a_1 is 3, a_2 is 8, a_3 is 13, and so on.

The nth term of the sequence is denoted by a_n.

A1 The formula for the nth term of the sequence a above is

$$a_n = 5n - 2.$$

Calculate the value of (a) a_4 (b) a_8 (c) a_{10} (d) a_{100}

A2 The formula for the nth term of a sequence b is $b_n = 7 - 3n$.

Calculate the value of (a) b_1 (b) b_2 (c) b_3 (d) b_{20}

A3 The nth term of a sequence t is given by the formula $t_n = \dfrac{n(n+1)}{2}$.

Calculate t_1, t_2, t_3, t_4 and t_5. What is this sequence called?

A4 The first four terms of an arithmetic sequence u are
$u_1 = 5, \quad u_2 = 9, \quad u_3 = 13, \quad u_4 = 17$

Work out a formula for the nth term and write it in the form $u_n = \ldots$

A5 The first four terms of a geometric sequence v are
$v_1 = 4, \quad v_2 = 20, \quad v_3 = 100, \quad v_4 = 500.$

Work out a formula for v_n.

A6 The nth term of a sequence h is given by the formula $h_n = \dfrac{1}{n}$.

(a) Use a calculator to work out h_{70} as a decimal, to 5 d.p.

(b) Which is the first term of the sequence to be less than 0·0001?

B Flowcharts

A **flowchart** can be used to give instructions for calculating the terms
of a sequence one after the other.
A flowchart of this kind uses the term-to-term rule for the sequence.

B1   This flowchart gives instructions for producing a sequence
$a_1, a_2, a_3, \ldots$ up as far as a_8.

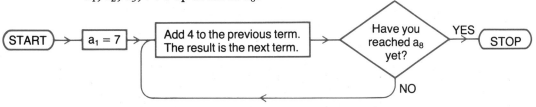

Write out the values of $a_1, a_2, \ldots$ up to a_8.

In question B1, you went round and round the loop in the flowchart
until you got the answer 'yes' to the question.

Any process which consists of repeating the same set of instructions
again and again is called an **iterative** process.
('Iterum' is the Latin word for 'again'.)

B2   Write down the values of $b_1, b_2, \ldots$ produced by this flowchart.

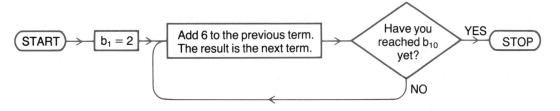

In question B2, you started with the value of b_1 and then added 6 to
get each next term. The pattern of calculation goes like this.

$$b_1 + 6 = b_2$$
$$b_2 + 6 = b_3$$
$$b_3 + 6 = b_4, \text{ and so on.}$$

We can use suffix notation to write a formula which shows how
you go from the nth term to the next one.

The term after the nth term will be the $(n+1)$th term, or b_{n+1}.

So the formula for going from the nth term to the $(n+1)$th term is

$$b_n + 6 = b_{n+1}$$

Don't make this look like $b_n + 1$.

For example, when n is 4 we get $b_4 + 6 = b_{4+1}$
                            or $b_4 + 6 = b_5$

87

B3 (a) Write down the values of $c_1, c_2, c_3, \ldots$ produced by this flowchart.

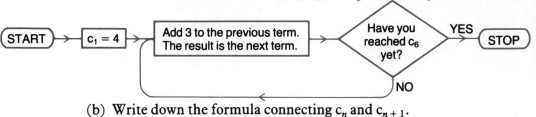

(b) Write down the formula connecting c_n and c_{n+1}.

B4 (a) Write down the values of $d_1, d_2, d_3, \ldots$ produced by this flowchart.

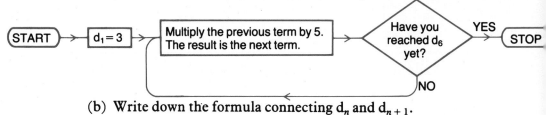

(b) Write down the formula connecting d_n and d_{n+1}.

B5 This flowchart gives instructions for producing a sequence $s_1, s_2, \ldots$ up to s_8.

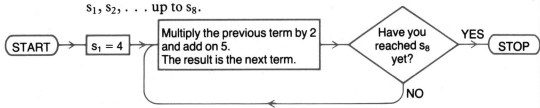

(a) Write down the values of $s_1, s_2, \ldots$ up to s_8.

(b) Write down the formula connecting s_n and s_{n+1}.

B6 The first term of a sequence is $u_1 = 7$.
The formula connecting u_n and u_{n+1} is $4u_n + 2 = u_{n+1}$.

Draw a flowchart for producing values of $u_1, u_2, \ldots$ up to u_{10}.

B7 (a) Write down the values of $v_1, v_2, \ldots$ produced by this flowchart.

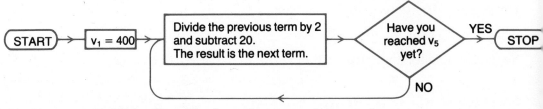

(b) Write down the formula connecting v_n and v_{n+1}.

C Two kinds of formula for a sequence

If we know the first term of a sequence, and we know the formula connecting the nth term and the $(n+1)$th term (the **iteration formula**), we can calculate the terms one by one.

For example, suppose the first term, a_1, of a sequence is 9, and the iteration formula connecting a_n and a_{n+1} is $3a_n - 1 = a_{n+1}$.

> This formula says:
> Multiply each term by 3 and subtract 1 to get the next term.

We can calculate $a_2, a_3, a_4, \ldots$, like this.

1 Put $n = 1$ in the iteration formula. We get $3a_1 - 1 = a_2$.

We know that a_1 is 9, so $3 \times 9 - 1 = a_2$, so $a_2 = 26$.

2 Put $n = 2$ in the iteration formula. We get $3a_2 - 1 = a_3$.

We know that a_2 is 26, so $3 \times 26 - 1 = a_3$, so $a_3 = 77$.

3 Put $n = 3$ in the iteration formula. And so on.

C1 The first term, b_1, of a sequence is 3.
The iteration formula connecting b_n and b_{n+1} is $2b_n + 1 = b_{n+1}$.

Calculate $b_2, b_3, b_4,$ and b_5.

C2 In a sequence u, the first term, u_1, is 10.
u_n and u_{n+1} are connected by the iteration formula

$$\frac{u_n}{2} + 1 = u_{n+1}.$$

(a) Calculate $u_2, u_3, u_4, \ldots$ up to u_{10}.

(b) What appears to happen to u_n as n gets larger and larger?

C3 In a sequence w, the first term, w_1, is 1 and the iteration formula connecting w_n and w_{n+1} is

$$\frac{3w_n + 1}{2} = w_{n+1}.$$

Calculate $w_2, w_3, \ldots$ up to w_6.

*C4 The iteration formula connecting the nth and the $(n+1)$th terms of a sequence z is $5z_n - 2 = z_{n+1}$. The value of z_6 is $^-312$.

Calculate the values of $z_1, z_2, \ldots$ up to z_5.

We have seen earlier that there are two different ways of giving the rules for calculating the terms of a sequence.

One way is to give the first term and the iteration formula for going from term to term.
For example, $s_1 = 7$ and $2s_n + 3 = s_{n+1}$.

The other way is to give the formula for calculating the nth term directly, without first having to calculate the previous terms.
For example, $t_n = 3n + 5$.

With the second type of formula, we can work out, say, the 50th term straight away. For example, $t_{50} = 3 \times 50 + 5 = 155$.
With the iteration formula, we can only work out the 50th term by first calculating the 2nd, 3rd, 4th, ... and so on.

Worked example

The first six terms of an arithmetic sequence are

a_1	a_2	a_3	a_4	a_5	a_6	...
3	10	17	24	31	38	...

(a) Find the iteration formula connecting a_n and a_{n+1}.
(b) Find the formula for a_n in terms of n.

(a) The term-to-term rule is 'add 7'. So the formula is $a_n + 7 = a_{n+1}$.

(b) To get from the first term to the nth term we have to add 7 a total of $(n-1)$ times. So $a_n = 3 + 7(n-1) = 3 + 7n - 7 = 7n - 4$.

Check: when n is 5, say, the formula gives $a_5 = 7 \times 5 - 4 = 31.$ ✓

C5 The first five terms of an arithmetic sequence are

b_1	b_2	b_3	b_4	b_5	...
8	11	14	17	20	...

(a) Find the iteration formula connecting b_n and b_{n+1}.

(b) Find the formula for b_n in terms of n.

C6 The first five terms of a geometric sequence are

c_1	c_2	c_3	c_4	c_5	...
4	20	100	500	2500	...

(a) Find the iteration formula connecting c_n and c_{n+1}.

(b) Find the formula for c_n in terms of n.

C7 The first term of a sequence u is $u_1 = 1$.
The iteration formula connecting u_n and u_{n+1} is $2u_n + 1 = u_{n+1}$.

(a) Calculate u_2, u_3, u_4, u_5 and u_6.

(b) Can you spot the formula for u_n in terms of n?

C8 Repeat question C7 for the sequence v where $v_1 = 1$ and $3v_n + 4 = v_{n+1}$

12 Exponential growth and decay

A Exponential growth and uniform growth

Many tiny organisms reproduce by splitting into two.

This diagram shows the growth of a population of organisms, starting with only one individual.

At the end of each minute, every existing organism splits into 2.

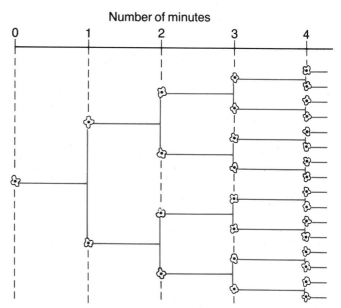

Number of minutes

A1 (a) How many organisms will there be after

(i) 5 minutes (ii) 8 minutes (iii) 10 minutes (iv) 15 minutes

(b) Write down a formula for the number of organisms after n minutes.

(c) After how many minutes will the population reach more than 1 million?

A2 Imagine an organism which splits into 3 at the end of each minute. To start with, there is just one individual.

(a) How many organisms will there be after

(i) 2 minutes (ii) 5 minutes (iii) 10 minutes (iv) n minutes

(b) After how many minutes will the population reach more than 1 million?

A3 An organism splits into 10 at the end of each minute. If there is one individual to start with, how many will there be after 5 minutes?

91

A waterweed is growing in a lake. The area covered by the weed
doubles during the course of each year.

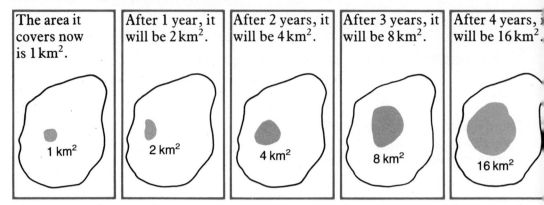

| The area it covers now is 1 km². | After 1 year, it will be 2 km². | After 2 years, it will be 4 km². | After 3 years, it will be 8 km². | After 4 years, it will be 16 km². |

Here is a graph showing the area covered. It makes sense to
draw a continuous curve because the area grows gradually
during the course of each year.

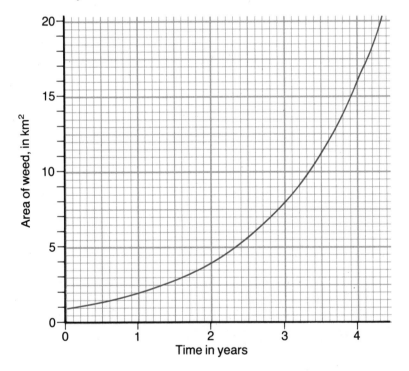

A4 (a) From the graph, find the area of weed 2·5 years from the start.

(b) Find the area 1 year later (3·5 years from the start).
Notice that the area doubled in the 1 year between
2·5 and 3·5 years.

(c) Check that the area doubles between any two times 1 year apart.

A quantity which grows by being multiplied by the same number in equal periods of time is said to grow **exponentially**.

The area of weed grows exponentially: it is multiplied by 2 in every period of 1 year.

Suppose a country's population is multiplied by 1·5 during every period of 10 years. Then the population grows exponentially.

Another kind of growth is where equal amounts are **added** in equal periods of time. This is called **uniform** growth.
For example, if a country's population goes up by 2 million in every period of 10 years, then it grows **uniformly**.

In the next question you will be comparing exponential growth and uniform growth.

A5 A, B and C are three countries. Each of them now has a population of 50 million.

Country A's population grows uniformly by 50 million in every period of 10 years.

Country B's population grows uniformly by 100 million in every period of 10 years.

Country C's population is multiplied by 1·5 during every period of 10 years.

(a) Copy and complete this table.

Number of years		0	10	20	30	40	50	60	70
Population in millions	A	50							
	B	50							
	C	50							

(b) Draw axes on graph paper. Suitable scales are

Across: 2 cm to 10 years   Up: 1 cm to 50 million

Draw the three population graphs on the same axes, and label them A, B and C.

(c) Notice that although population C grows more slowly at first than either A or B, its graph gets steeper and steeper.

From your graph find out when population C overtakes

(i) population A   (ii) population B

Another example of exponential growth is where a quantity is increased by the same **percentage** each year, or each month, etc.

Suppose you put £100 into a savings account, and the rate of interest is 6% per year. In each year your savings are multiplied by 1·06. This table shows how they grow.

Number of years	0	1	2	3	4	5
Amount in £	100	106	112·36	119·10	126·25	133·82

×1·06   ×1·06   and so on

A6   Find how long it will take for your savings to double when the rate of interest is 6% per year.

A7   You put £50 into a savings account. It earns interest at the rate of 13% per year.

(a) Make a table showing the amount in the account at the end of 1 year, 2 years, 3 years, and so on up to 6 years.

(b) You should find that after 6 years your savings have approximately doubled. After how many more years will they have doubled again?

A8   This table gives the population of India at the censuses in 1961, 1971 and 1981.

Year	Population
1961	439 072 582
1971	547 949 809
1981	683 880 051

(a) Calculate the percentage increase in the population between 1961 and 1971, to the nearest 1%.

(b) Calculate the percentage increase between 1971 and 1981, to the nearest 1%.

(c) If the population continues to grow by the same percentage every 10 years, calculate an estimate for the population in 1991, 2001 and 2011.

A9   If a small population of organisms, such as bacteria, is placed in a container, the population usually grows exponentially at first. If the food supply is limited, some organisms die and the population grows more and more slowly. Eventually it reaches a maximum size, for which the food supply is just sufficient.

Sketch a graph showing the growth of the population.

B Exponential decay

When a quantity grows exponentially, it is multiplied by the same number in equal periods of time. The multiplier is greater than 1.

When the multiplier is less than 1, we get **exponential decay**.

For example, suppose a population of insects decreases by 8% every year. The population at the end of a year is 92%, or 0·92 of what it was at the start of the year. So the multiplier in this case is 0·92.

If the original population is 10 000, the population after 1 year, 2 years, 3 years, and so on is as shown in this table.

Number of years	0	1	2	3	4	5
Population	10 000	9200	8464	7787	7164	6591

×0·92   ×0·92   and so on

B1 (a) Continue the table above. Calculate the population after 6 years and after 7 years.

    (b) Find out how long it will take for the population to fall to less than half of what it was to start with.

B2 The manufacturer of a machine for drying grain claims that 10 minutes in the machine will remove 65% of the moisture.

Suppose a load of grain contains 5000 g of moisture. Copy and complete this table, together with the value of the multiplier. (It is **not** 0·65.)

Time in machine, in minutes	0	10	20	30	40
Amount of moisture, in g	5000				

× ...   × ...   × ...   × ...

B3 1 litre of salt solution contains 50 g of dissolved salt. One half of the solution is poured away, so that 25 g of salt remains in 0·5 litre of solution. The remaining solution is then made up to 1 litre with water, so that now 1 litre of solution contains 25 g of salt.

The process of dilution is repeated again and again. Each time half the solution is poured away and then the rest is 'topped up' to 1 litre. Copy and complete this table.

Number of dilutions	0	1	2	3	4	5
Mass of salt, in g	50					

B4 Repeat question B3, but with $\frac{1}{4}$ of the solution being poured away each time. Start with 50 g of salt in 1 litre of solution.

C Negative indices

Think back to the waterweed whose area doubles during the course of 1 year. To start with, the area is 1 km^2.

After 1 year, the area is 2 km^2.
After 2 years, it is 4, or 2^2 km^2.
After 3 years, it is 8, or 2^3 km^2.

Let $A \text{ km}^2$ be the area after t years. Then A and t are connected by the formula $A = 2^t$.

Here is a table of values of A and t.

t (time in years)	0	1	2	3	4	5
A (area in km²)	1	2	4	8	16	32

Now think what the area must have been 1 year **before** the start. It must have been $\frac{1}{2} \text{ km}^2$, because the area doubles during each year.

So 2 years before the start it must have been $\frac{1}{4} \text{ km}^2$.

3 years before the start it must have been $\frac{1}{8} \text{ km}^2$, and so on.

So we can extend the table backwards, like this.

4 years before 0.

t (time in years) ...	$^-4$	$^-3$	$^-2$	$^-1$	0	1	2	3	4	5
A (area in km²) ...	$\frac{1}{16}$	$\frac{1}{8}$	$\frac{1}{4}$	$\frac{1}{2}$	1	2	4	8	16	32

We know that the formula $A = 2^t$ is true at the right-hand end of the table. For example, when t is 3, $A = 2^3 = 8$.

If we want the formula to be true for the whole table, then
2^0 **must mean 1**, 2^{-1} **must mean** $\frac{1}{2}$, 2^{-2} **must mean** $\frac{1}{4}$, and so on.

Notice that 2^{-1} is equal to $\frac{1}{2^1}$, 2^{-2} is equal to $\frac{1}{2^2}$, and so on.

C1 Write these as fractions.

(a) 2^{-4} (b) 2^{-5} (c) 2^{-7} (d) 2^{-10} (e) 2^{-11}

C2 In this table, A and t are connected by the formula $A = 3^t$.

t					0	1	2	3	4	5
A						3	9	27	81	243

(a) Copy the table and extend it backwards so that t goes down to $^-4$.

(b) Write as a fraction (i) 3^{-5} (ii) 3^{-6} (iii) 3^{-7}

Negative powers of 10 are used to write numbers less than 1 in **standard index form**.

10^{-1} means $\frac{1}{10}$, 10^{-2} means $\frac{1}{10^2}$ or $\frac{1}{100}$, and so on.

The decimal places in a number can be labelled with negative powers of 10, like this.

$$\begin{array}{cccccc} & 10^{-1} & 10^{-2} & 10^{-3} & 10^{-4} & 10^{-5} & \ldots \\ 0 \cdot & 0 & 0 & 6 & 3 & 7 \end{array}$$

In standard index form, the number above is $6{\cdot}37 \times 10^{-3}$.

C3 Write each of these as a negative power of 10.

(a) $\frac{1}{1000}$ (b) $\frac{1}{10000}$ (c) $0{\cdot}01$ (d) $0{\cdot}00001$ (e) $0{\cdot}0000001$

C4 Write each of these as a fraction and as a decimal.

(a) 10^{-2} (b) 10^{-6} (c) 10^{-7} (d) 10^{-10}

C5 Write these numbers in standard index form.

(a) $0{\cdot}04$ (b) $0{\cdot}043$ (c) $0{\cdot}0432$ (d) $0{\cdot}0000683$

(e) $0{\cdot}652$ (f) $730{\cdot}6$ (g) 953000 (h) $0{\cdot}00862$

(i) $23{\cdot}008$ (j) $0{\cdot}0085$ (k) $0{\cdot}982$ (l) 137000000

The general rule for negative powers is this: a^{-n} means the same as $\frac{1}{a^n}$.

C6 Work these out as fractions

(a) 4^{-2} (b) 4^{-1} (c) 4^{-3} (d) $2^{-2} \times 3^{-2}$ (e) 5^{-3} (f) 3^{-5}

C7 A dish of boiling water is taken from a gas ring.
The temperature, $\theta\,°C$, of the water afterwards is given by the formula

$$\theta = 80(2^{-t}) + 20.$$

t is the time in minutes since the dish was removed from the ring.

(a) Copy and complete this table.

t	0	1	2	3	4	5
θ						

(b) Draw a graph of (t, θ).
Use it to estimate θ when t is $3{\cdot}5$.

(c) According to the formula, what happens to θ as t gets larger and larger?

7 Sequences (1)

7.1 Find a formula for the nth term of each of these arithmetic sequences:
(a) 5, 12, 19, 26, 33, 40, . . .
(b) 19, 15, 11, 7, 3, $^-1$, . . .

7.2 Find a formula for the nth term of this geometric sequence:
    4, 12, 36, 108, 324, 972, . . .

7.3 Can you spot a formula for the nth term of each of these sequences?

(a)
Position	1	2	3	4	5	6	...
Term	2	5	10	17	26	37	...

(b)
Position	1	2	3	4	5	6	...
Term	300	150	100	75	60	50	...

(c)
Position	1	2	3	4	5	6	...
Term	1	3	7	15	31	63	...

8 Types of proportionality

8.1 In an electroplating process, the amount of copper deposited in one hour is proportional to the strength of the current.

When the current is 15·5 amps, the mass deposited is 36·7 g.

(a) Calculate the mass deposited when the current is 10 amps.
(b) Calculate the strength of the current needed to deposit 50 g of copper in one hour.

8.2 The density of a sample of a gas is inversely proportional to its volume. When the volume is 2·4 m³, the density is 1·4 kg/m³. Calculate

(a) the density when the volume is 1·5 m³
(b) the volume when the density is 0·4 kg/m³

8.3 The amount of energy stored in a rotating flywheel is proportional to the square of the speed of rotation.

What happens to the amount of energy when the speed of rotation is
(a) doubled   (b) divided by 4   ★(c) increased by 20%

8.4 Nadim measured the diameter, d mm, and the mass, m grams, of several ball bearings. Here are the measurements.

d	5	10	12	15	16	20
m	0·5	4·1	7·2	14·0	16·9	33·1

(a) Draw a graph of (d, m)

(b) Is m proportional to d?

(c) Make a new table showing values of d^2 and m. Draw a graph of (d^2, m). Is m proportional to d^2?

(d) Draw a graph of (d^3, m). Is m proportional to d^3?

8.5 When you look out to sea the distance of the visible horizon is proportional to the square root of your own height above sea level.

From a height of 50 feet you can see 8·6 miles. How far will you be able to see if you
(a) double your height   (b) go up to a height of 200 feet

8.6 If $Q \propto P^2$, and Q is 43·6 when P is 2·8, calculate Q when P is 7·2.

9 Manipulating formulas

9.1 If $s = p^2 m$ and $p = \dfrac{v}{m}$, find a formula for s in terms of v and m.

9.2 If $k = \dfrac{p}{q}$ and $q = \dfrac{r}{p}$, find a formula for k in terms of p and r.

9.3 If $y = a - bx$ and $x = b - az$, find a formula for
(a) y in terms of a, b and z (eliminating x)
(b) y in terms of a, x and z (eliminating b)

9.4 Re-arrange the formula $v^2 = u^2 + 2as$ to make a the subject.

9.5 Re-arrange each of these formulas to make p the subject.

(a) $q = k\sqrt{p}$ (b) $q = \sqrt{(kp)}$ (c) $q = \sqrt{\left(\dfrac{p}{k}\right)}$ (d) $q = \dfrac{\sqrt{p}}{k}$

(e) $q = \dfrac{k}{\sqrt{p}}$ (f) $q = \sqrt{\left(\dfrac{k}{p}\right)}$ (g) $q = \sqrt{(k + p)}$ (h) $q = \sqrt{(k - p)}$

10 Probability

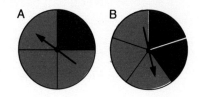

10.1 These two spinners are spun.

Calculate the probability of getting

(a) black on A and black on B

(b) red on A and red on B

(c) black on one spinner and red on the other (either way round)

10.2 Spinner B in question 10.1 is spun twice.

(a) Copy this tree diagram and complete it by filling in the missing probabilities.

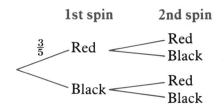

1st spin   2nd spin

$\frac{3}{5}$ Red — Red / Black

Black — Red / Black

(b) Calculate the probability that both spins give black.

(c) Calculate the probability of getting one red and one black in either order.

10.3 A box contains 6 black balls and 3 white balls.
Two balls are taken out at random.
Draw a tree diagram and use it to calculate the probability that

(a) both balls taken out are black

(b) both balls are white   (c) one is black and one is white

10.4 A single telephone line serves two phones A and B. At any particular moment there is a 70% chance that A is engaged and a 60% chance that B is engaged. The two phones are used independently of each other.

What is the probability that at least one of the phones is engaged?

11 Sequences (2)

11.1 The nth term of a sequence is given by the formula $a_n = \dfrac{n(n + 3)}{2}$.

Calculate the value of (a) a_4 (b) a_{40} (c) a_{57}

11.2 Calculate the first five terms of the sequence b, where $b_n = \dfrac{2n + 3}{n}$.

11.3 A sequence s is generated by this flowchart.

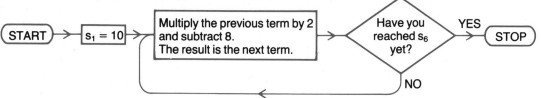

(a) Work out the values of s_2, s_3, s_4, s_5 and s_6.

(b) Write down the formula connecting s_n and s_{n+1}.

11.4 In a sequence r, the first term r_1 is 6, and the formula connecting r_n and r_{n+1} is

$$\frac{24}{r_n} - 2 = r_{n+1}.$$

Calculate the values of r_2, r_3, . . . up to r_6.

12 Exponential growth and decay

12.1 Jane's salary rises by £600 at the end of each year. Her brother Michael's salary is increased by 10% at the end of each year.

They start work together at a salary of £5000 each for the first year.

Make a table showing their salaries for the 2nd, 3rd, 4th, . . . years, and find out which is the first year in which Michael's salary is bigger than Jane's.

12.2 The population of a colony of wild animals is estimated to be falling at the rate of 12% per year.

This year's population is estimated to be 5000.

Calculate estimates for the population 1 year from now, 2 years from now, and so on, and find out when the population will fall to less than half its present size.

12.3 You are talking to someone who has never met negative indices before. (He or she knows about positive indices.)

How would you explain why it is that a^{-2} means the same as $\dfrac{1}{a^2}$?

12.4 Calculate each of these as a fraction.

(a) 3^{-3} (b) 5^{-2} (c) $3^{-2} \times 4^{-1}$ (d) $\dfrac{1}{2^{-3}}$ (e) $\dfrac{3^{-1}}{2^{-1}}$

13 Optimisation

A Minimising

A and B are two cities.
The land on which B is built has firm rock underneath it.
The land on which A is built is less firm clay.

The boundary between the firm ground and the clay is shown on the map.

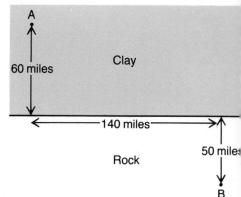

A road is to be built between A and B.
The cost of building the road is £2 million per mile on the firm ground and £3 million per mile on the clay.

The problem is to choose a route for the road which will make the cost of building it as small as possible.

We say we want to **minimise** the cost of building the road.

A1   Draw the map showing the positions of A, B and the boundary to a scale of 1 cm to 10 miles.

(a) Someone suggests that the part of the road built on clay should be made as small as possible, because this is the most expensive part to build.

Mark this route on your map. C is the point where this route crosses the boundary.

Measure each part of the route and work out the cost of building the road along this route.

(b) Someone else suggests that it would be better to cross the boundary at a point 20 miles from C as shown here.

Mark this route on your map, and calculate the cost of building the road along it.

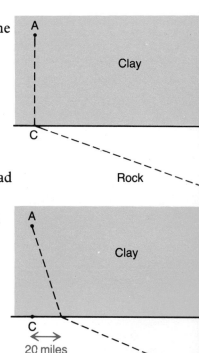

(c) Calculate the cost of building the road when the point where it crosses the boundary is 40 miles, 60 miles, 80 miles, and 100 miles from C.

Enter the results in a table.

Distance of crossing point from C, in miles	0	20	40	60	80	100
Cost of road, in £ million						

(d) Draw axes using the scales shown here.

Plot the points from your table, and draw a smooth curve through them.

(e) Estimate from your graph where the route should cross the boundary if the cost of building the road is to be minimised.

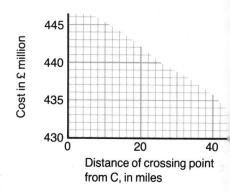

Distance of crossing point from C, in miles

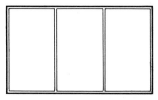

A2 A factory makes window frames like the one on the left. The frames are made from aluminium strip.

There are four uprights and two cross pieces.

A builder orders windows in this style. He says he wants each window to have a total area of $4\,m^2$.

(a) Suppose the height of the window is $1\cdot20\,m$. Calculate the width in metres to 2 d.p., and explain why the total length of aluminium strip is $11\cdot46\,m$.

(b) Copy and complete this table.

Height in m	1·20	1·30	1·40	1·50	1·60	1·70
Width in m	3·33					
Total length of strip, in m	11·46					

(c) Draw axes using the scales shown here.

Plot the points from the table, and draw a smooth curve through them.

(d) Estimate from your graph the height of the window which minimises the length of aluminium strip needed.

(e) How wide will this window be?

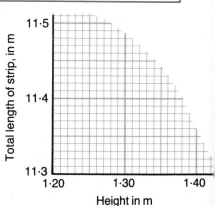

Total length of strip, in m

Height in m

A3 A manufacturer makes heated towel rails out of chrome-plated copper tube.

They all have two uprights and three cross-bars like this.

A customer asks for one which has a 'usable area' of $1\,m^2$.

She means the coloured area has to be $1\,m^2$.

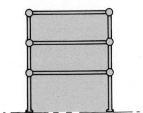

The manufacturer wants to minimise the amount of tube used.

(a) If the rail is made $0\cdot70\,m$ wide, calculate its height and the total length of tube needed to make it.

(b) Copy and complete this table.

Width in m	0·70	0·80	0·90	1·00	1·10	1·20
Height in m						
Total length of tube, in m						

(c) Draw axes on graph paper with 'width' across and 'total length of tube' up. Choose your own scales so as to make good use of the graph paper.

Plot the points from your table and draw a smooth curve through them.

(d) Estimate from your graph the width of the rail which minimises the length of tube used.

A4 A machine cuts out complicated shapes. It will work at any rate between 5 shapes per hour and 100 shapes per hour.

The machine operator is paid £10 per hour.

An order comes in for 1000 shapes.

(a) What will be the cost of paying the operator if the 1000 shapes are made at a rate of 5 shapes per hour?

(b) What will be the cost of paying the operator if the 1000 shapes are made at 100 per hour?

It seems cheapest to run the machine at its fastest rate. However, the cutting blades and other parts of the machine suffer more wear the faster the machine goes.

An engineer estimates that the cost in pounds of replacing blades and parts on a job of this size is 20 times the rate, in shapes per hour, at which it is working.

(c) What will the replacement cost be if the machine works at 5 shapes per hour?

(d) What will they be if it works at 100 shapes per hour?

(e) Copy and complete the table below to find out the total cost of the job for different rates of working.

Number of shapes per hour	Hours taken	Cost of paying operator	Repair costs	Total cost
5	200	£2000	£100	£2100
10				
20				
30				
40				
50				
60				

(f) Draw axes with the number of shapes per hour across and the total cost up.
Plot the points from your table. Draw a smooth curve through them.

(g) Estimate the rate of working which minimises the total cost.

(h) Check your estimate by calculation like this.
First calculate the total cost of making 1000 shapes at your estimated rate of working.
Then add 3 to your estimated rate and re-calculate the total cost.
Then subtract 3 from your estimated rate and do the same.

If the total cost at your estimated rate is less than at the slightly lower and higher rates, your estimate is a good one.

We can use algebra to write a formula connecting the total cost with the rate of working of the machine in question A4. Question A5 shows how.

A5 Let r be the rate of working, in shapes per hour, of the machine in question A4.

(a) Write down an expression, in terms of r, for

(i) the number of hours it will take to make 1000 shapes

(ii) the cost in pounds of paying the operator, who is paid £10 per hour

(iii) the repair costs in pounds, which are 20 times the rate, in shapes per hour, at which the machine works

(b) Let T be the total cost in pounds. Write down a formula for T in terms of r. Check that it gives the correct value of T when $r = 5$.

B Maximising

Suppose we have a piece of tinplate 30 cm by 30 cm.

We want to make a square cake tin out of it.
We do it by cutting out the shaded pieces and bending upwards along the dotted lines.

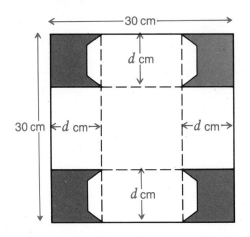

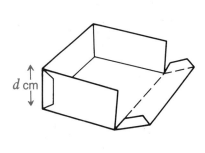

Let d cm be the depth of the cake tin.

If we make d small, we will get a shallow cake tin.

If we make d large, we will get a tall, narrow tin.

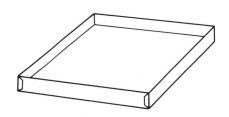

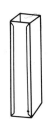

Suppose we want to **maximise** the volume of the tin.
(In other words, we want to make the volume as large as possible.)

Let V cm^3 be the volume of the tin.
We need to know how V is related to d, so we need to find a formula for V in terms of d.

Look at the diagram of the flat piece of tinplate.
The base of the tin is the dotted square in the middle.

The length of each side of the base is $(30 - 2d)$ cm.

So the area of the base is $(30 - 2d)^2$ cm^2.

The volume of the tin is equal to area of base × depth.

So $V = (30 - 2d)^2 \times d$, which we can write $V = d(30 - 2d)^2$.

B1 (a) Use the formula $V = d(30 - 2d)^2$ to find the value of V when d is 0, 2, 4, 6, 8, 10, 12 and 14.

For example, when d is 4, $\quad V = 4(30 - 8)^2$
$$= 4 \times 22^2$$
$$= 4 \times 484 = 1936.$$
Make a table of values of d and V.

(b) Draw a graph of (d, V).

(c) From your graph estimate the value of d which maximises V.

(d) Use your estimated value of d to calculate the maximum value of V.

B2 This time the original piece of tinplate is a rectangle 30 cm by 20 cm.

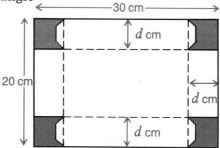

(a) Find a formula for V in terms of d.

(b) Use the formula to find V when d is 0, 2, 4, 6, 8 and 10. Make a table of values of d and V.

(c) Draw a graph of (d, V).

(d) Estimate the value of d which maximises V.

(e) Use your estimate to calculate the maximum value of V.

C Optimisation

Optimising means choosing the best thing to do.
'Best' may mean 'cheapest', 'quickest', 'largest', 'smallest', and so on, depending on the circumstances.

What is 'best' depends on your point of view. If a driver has a long journey to do, she may think it best to get to where she is going as quickly as possible. If so, she will travel at the fastest possible speed. But at a fast speed the car uses up petrol at a greater rate, so that will be more expensive than going at a slower speed. Only the driver herself can decide whether time or money is more valuable to her.

C1 Nisha has to drive from Sheffield to Exeter, a distance of 240 miles. Her car is getting old. This table shows the number of miles per gallon it will do at various speeds.

Speed	30 m.p.h.	40 m.p.h.	50 m.p.h.	60 m.p.h.	70 m.p.h.
Miles per gallon	25	30	25	20	15

(a) If Nisha travels at 30 m.p.h. her car will do 25 miles per gallon. How many gallons of petrol will she use up on the journey of 240 miles if she goes at 30 m.p.h.?

(b) Petrol costs £2 per gallon. How much will the petrol for the journey cost?

(c) Calculate the petrol costs for the journey when the speed is 40 m.p.h., 50 m.p.h., 60 m.p.h. and 70 m.p.h. Make a table to show them.

(d) If petrol costs were all that mattered, which speed should Nisha travel at?

(e) Nisha is a photographer. If she were not driving she would be working and earning £5 per hour. So every hour she spends driving costs her £5 in lost income.

If she does the 240-mile journey at a speed of 30 m.p.h., how long will the journey take, and what is the cost of that time at the rate of £5 per hour?

(f) Work out the 'time cost' for the journey when the speed is 40 m.p.h., 50 m.p.h., 60 m.p.h. and 70 m.p.h. Make a table.

(g) If Nisha wants to minimise the total cost of the journey, at which of the five speeds should she travel? Show how you get your answer.

C2 When this book was printed, it cost a lot of money just to set up the printing machine, even before any copies were printed. Then when printing did begin, the paper, printing and binding had to be paid for.

Here are some typical costs for producing a book.

Cost of setting up machine	£500
Cost of paper, printing and binding	£450 per 1000 copies

(a) What would the **total** cost be if the printer does 4000 copies?

(b) Divide your answer to (a) by 4000 to get the **cost per copy**.

(c) What would be the total cost of producing 8000 copies?

(d) What would the cost per copy be in this case? Give your answer to the nearest £0·001.

(Continued on next page.)

108

(e) Copy and complete this table.

Number of copies printed	Setting-up cost	Cost of paper, printing, binding	Total production cost	Production cost per copy
4000	£500	£1800	£2300	£0·575
6000				
8000				
10 000				
12 000				
14 000				

(f) If you want the production cost per copy to be as low as possible, what seems to be the best way to achieve this?

In practice, things are more complicated, because storing books costs money. If you print a lot of books, they will not all be sold at once, and some will need to be stored until they are sold.

Suppose the books are likely to be sold at a rate of 2000 per year.
The books are stored in containers, each of which holds 2000 copies.

Suppose you print **8000 copies**.

So you need 4 containers for the 1st year, 3 for the 2nd, 2 for the 3rd and 1 for the 4th.

The cost of using a container for 1 year is **£50**, so storage costs will be $(4 + 3 + 2 + 1) \times £50 = 10 \times £50 = £500$.

This is the storage cost when 8000 copies are printed, so the storage cost **per copy** is $\frac{£500}{8000} = £0·063$ (to the nearest £0·001).

(g) Copy and complete this table. The first two columns are the same as the first and last columns of the previous table.

Number of copies printed	Production cost per copy	Storage cost per copy	Total cost per copy
4000			
6000			
8000	£0·513	£0·063	£0·576
and so on			

(h) Which number of copies will minimise the total cost per copy of production and storage?

109

14 Sampling

A Representative samples

Every so often, especially near to elections and by-elections, newspapers publish the results of opinion polls.

Here is the result of an opinion poll carried out in a constituency about a week before a by-election. People were asked which party they intended to vote for.

> ## By-election: **Labour narrows the gap**.
>
> The results of the latest opinion poll put the Conservatives only 5 per cent ahead of Labour. The full results of the poll are
>
> | | |
> |---|---|
> | Conservative | 38% |
> | Labour | 33% |
> | Liberal/SDP | 21% |
> | Don't know | 8% |

The size of the electorate (the total number of people entitled to vote) was 40 000. It would be very expensive to try to ask everybody, so the pollsters asked 1000 people how they would vote. The results above are based on the answers of those 1000 people.

There were 39 000 people who were not asked. So how can the poll results be of any use in telling us how the whole electorate would vote?

They can only be useful if the 1000 people are typical, or, as we say, a **representative sample** of the whole electorate.

It would be no good asking 1000 people who all live in large houses in the most expensive part of the constituency, or 1000 people who are all over 70 years old, or 1000 people who are all unemployed. The voting behaviour of special groups like these may not be typical of the whole electorate.

110

Biassed samples

One of the most famous mistakes in opinion sampling was made in the USA in 1936. That year there was an election for president, with two candidates: a Democrat (F.D. Roosevelt) and a Republican (A.E. Landon).

A magazine carried out an opinion poll in which over 2 million people were asked how they would vote. The results seemed to show that the Republican would win easily. But in fact the Democrat won.

The opinion pollsters picked their sample of voters from telephone directories and lists of car owners. At that time, only people who were well-off had a telephone or car, and most well-off people voted Republican. Poorer people, who mostly voted Democrat, were not represented in the sample. We say the sample was **biassed** towards the richer, Republican, voters.

Questions for discussion

A publisher wants to know what percentage of the people in a town read novels. An interviewer is sent out to ask a sample of people whether they have read a novel in the past four weeks.

A1   Why would the interviewer be unlikely to get a representative sample of people if she stands outside the public library and asks people coming out?

A2   Would she be likely to get a representative sample by asking people in the High Street between 10 and 11 a.m. on a weekday? If not, why not?

A3   Suppose she stands outside the railway station and asks people coming home from work. Would she be likely to get a representative sample? If not, why not?

A4   Can you suggest a way in which she could get a representative sample?

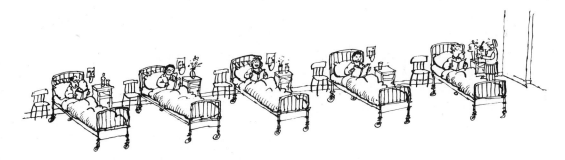

B Estimating the size of a population by sampling

You need an ordinary dice.

This is an aerial view of a piece of countryside showing the positions of trees.

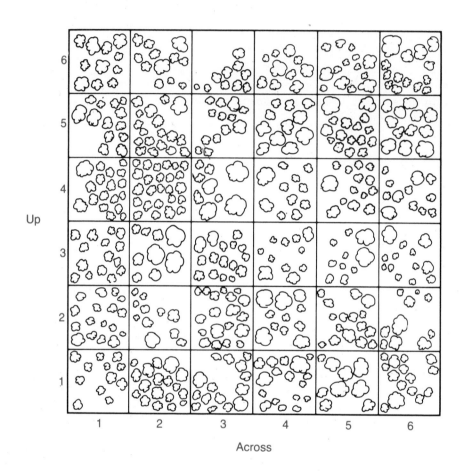

An agriculturalist wants to estimate the total number of trees.
She doesn't have the time (or patience) to count every single tree.

She has divided the area into 36 squares. She wants to estimate the total number of trees by choosing 9 representative squares and counting the trees in those 9 squares. She gets her estimate of the total by multiplying by 4.

B1 **Class activity**

    (a) Each member of the class chooses 9 squares which they think are 'representative' of all the squares. Write down the 'across' and 'up' numbers of each square that you choose.

    (b) Count the trees in your 9 squares. (Do not mark the diagram when you count. If you want to mark the trees, put a piece of tracing paper over the diagram.)

    (c) Multiply your number of trees by 4, to get your estimate of the total number of trees.

    (d) The teacher draws a number line on the board and each person's estimate is marked on it.

    Look at the overall spread of the estimates. Your teacher will tell you what the actual total number of trees is.

    (e) Discuss the ways in which people chose their 'representative' samples.

It is not all that easy to choose squares which are 'representative' of all the squares. One way of doing it is to leave the choice to **chance**, so that every square has an equal chance of being chosen to be in the sample.

A sample chosen in this way is called a **random sample**. In random sampling, the choice of sample is decided by tossing coins, throwing dice, or any other way of producing a chance result.

We can choose a random sample of 9 squares by throwing dice. The throws are done in pairs: in each pair, the first throw gives the number **across** and the second throw the number **up**. We carry on throwing until we have chosen 9 squares. (If the same square gets chosen twice, we throw again to get a different square.)

B2 **Class activity**

    Each person uses a dice to get a random sample of 9 squares. Estimate the total number of trees from your sample.

    Look at the spread of these estimates and compare it with the previous spread.

    Looking at the class's results as a whole, are the estimates obtained by random sampling any worse than those obtained by trying to choose 'representative' squares?

C Using random sequences

This drawing shows part of a collection of felled trees.
There are 100 trees altogether.

Each tree has a reference number. These numbers
go from 00 to 99.

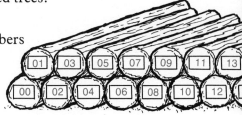

Suppose you want to estimate the total volume of timber in the 100 trees.
It is inconvenient and time-consuming to measure the volume of every
tree, so you are going to choose a random sample of 20 trees.

To understand how this can be done, you need to know about
random sequences.

Random sequences

Imagine a spinner with 10 equal parts, numbered from 0 to 9.
When this spinner is spun again and again, we get a sequence
of digits, for example

   5   0   6   3   7   9   4   7   1   6   5   1 ...

In this sequence it is not possible to predict what the next digit will be.
It is equally likely to be 0, 1, 2, 3, 4, 5, 6, 7, 8 or 9. We call such
a sequence a **random sequence** of digits.

In a very long random sequence of digits, the relative frequency of
each digit is the same. About $\frac{1}{10}$ will be 0, about $\frac{1}{10}$ will be 1, and so on.

Some electronic calculators have a **random number generator** on them,
and most computers can be programmed to generate random digits.
The digits may be produced in groups of two, three or four, for example

   409   789   068   457   449   859   886   213   270 ...

If you do not have a computer, or a calculator capable of generating
random sequences, you can use a **random number table**. This is
just a table of numbers which have been produced by a random
number generator. There is a table of this kind on the opposite page.

How to use a random number table

You can use the table to generate many different random sequences.
You have to decide where to start and what rule to follow for going
through the table. For example, you could decide to

   start at the top right-hand corner of the table, and
   go down the column of single digits and up the next, and so on.

This would give a sequence starting   6   4   5   5   0   2   3   1   2 ...

5568	0813	9599	8781	7973	8801	0529	0060	4049	6477	1818	6321	5996
1570	2557	3603	9014	7268	9575	4471	3283	0521	5984	7320	7848	0614
5392	9184	1587	9829	7587	8451	7862	5077	5683	9062	6982	5722	9495
0282	2355	1630	9600	3494	1785	3437	1136	8557	2139	6532	9081	9835
2784	4079	6617	7649	5164	7169	8351	7303	3814	8156	8224	6239	4950
2848	6085	0016	5328	4591	2931	7557	0680	6782	1311	4861	1825	8102
4236	5293	2612	9972	4985	1876	0309	2511	9500	0750	4930	0501	3833
0421	1509	0166	4833	0972	5984	8486	4816	3981	5635	4077	7131	8071
0697	3993	6510	6562	3127	3206	5709	3722	3271	4458	7487	2819	2772
7426	5641	5306	9213	7695	0360	4146	6075	1573	2914	4406	4045	7770
3117	2065	2957	8777	8113	4243	5186	5530	4552	8780	4093	2222	0079
7992	4354	9030	9163	3384	8334	0713	5966	3315	2931	8004	5741	2703
9737	9507	8963	2469	8676	3540	5132	5927	0139	8917	2272	2971	9118
6292	0501	6793	7425	2791	7831	7833	0214	7858	7046	3268	2960	1569
4298	3588	9412	6191	1451	4694	7662	3585	3867	6988	1616	5162	9188
5922	2767	4329	7878	3908	1288	9550	7976	1554	4763	7157	3713	3336
0019	0364	9448	7794	1799	4694	1530	2245	4507	8156	5165	0993	6250
7725	2356	4228	0747	9293	2972	1402	2226	9373	7008	7955	0872	9353
2247	7495	5486	1989	9966	1065	3017	1506	1978	4541	9156	5275	7878
7507	3723	8208	4632	3393	9290	1089	2540	2318	2979	0611	4528	8370
1680	2231	8846	5418	0498	5245	7071	2597	2268	0932	1882	4466	8450
1958	0382	9064	3511	7001	6239	6110	0613	1180	2624	9274	7598	0050
5417	8950	4530	2895	5605	9740	6827	6130	8353	3203	6493	9449	9206
1736	3480	4995	8567	7469	1505	3499	3957	2237	7623	1323	2943	4795
7630	2759	0496	0472	8906	6029	3547	0198	1369	3492	6785	0730	0001
5420	3648	8794	3712	1533	3950	4341	5840	4200	3840	8523	9025	6138
7920	9186	6596	1243	3426	6852	5140	5044	2807	7905	1860	8934	2387
0873	6060	1720	0047	3582	0639	6730	7649	7505	2484	9261	3539	5832
0899	3037	5554	2229	9341	6729	5380	2443	3650	7521	4615	3188	6012
3629	4605	8125	6880	6463	5349	7979	4525	5958	9010	1808	6708	9884

Estimating the total volume of timber by random sampling

Your teacher has a list of the volumes of each of the 100 trees.
(Of course, in practice these volumes would not be known by anyone,
otherwise sampling would be unnecessary! But the purpose of this work
is to let you see how close your estimates are to the actual total volume.)

C1 **Class activity**

(a) Each person uses the random number table to produce a random
sequence of 40 digits. Write them in pairs, for example

47 73 12 09 06 64 55 ...

If a pair is repeated, ignore the repeat and continue until
you have 20 different two-digit numbers.

(b) Your 20 numbers are the reference numbers of the trees in
your random sample. Your teacher will read out the volumes
of all the trees. Listen for those trees which are in your sample
and write down their volumes.

(c) Use the information about your sample to estimate the total
volume of the 100 trees.

(d) Mark everybody's estimates on a number line on the board and
compare the estimates with the actual total, which your teacher
will tell you.

D Sampling from a large population

Suppose we want to know the mean height of the fifteen-year-old boys in a school, and we do not have the time to measure every boy. We can choose a sample of the boys, and make an estimate from our sample.

We would want our sample to be representative. A safe way is to choose a random sample. But what should be the size of the sample?

If there are, say, 120 fifteen-year-old boys in the school, would a sample of 10 be sufficient to get a reliable estimate of the mean height? Or is there too great a risk that the 10 boys chosen might include a few exceptionally tall or exceptionally short boys and so be unrepresentative?

In the work which follows you will be finding out in a practical way how reliable sampling can be. You will be taking samples from a very large population of people in order to estimate the mean height, mean weight, etc. of that population.

The actual values of these various means are known to your teacher, so you will be able to find out how reliable are the estimates which you get from your samples.

For the work which follows you need the Database card and the random number table (worksheet Y4–1) which goes with it.

The Database card

The Database card contains two databases, called G and B.

Database G contains information about all the fourth-year girls in two neighbouring comprehensive schools.

Database B contains information about all the fourth-year boys in the two schools.

Each girl or boy in each database has a three-digit reference number (from 000 to 194 for the girls, and from 000 to 208 for the boys).

Some of the information is of a simple 'yes-or-no' kind. For example 'can he or she roll their tongue?'[1] In these cases, 1 means 'yes' and 0 'no'.

The measurements of height, waist, etc. are all in centimetres. 'Armspan' means this: ——— 'Handspan' means this:

'Head' means 'head circumference, measured just above the eyebrows'. The weights are in kilograms.

(The information in the databases was collected in February 1983.)

---

[1] This is something people either can or can't do. 'Rolling your tongue' means making it do this.

E Estimating a mean

E1 Question for discussion

What size of sample do you think will be necessary to get a reasonably reliable estimate of the mean height of the girls in database G? (There are 195 girls in the database.)

For the next activities you need database G and the random number table. The table has random three-digit numbers from 000 to 249.

E2 Class activity

We will start by seeing what happens when we choose a sample of size 5.

(a) Each person chooses a starting point in the random number table and a rule to follow. He or she then generates a random sample of five different girls' reference numbers.

(If one of the numbers you get is over 194, ignore it and continue. If you get a number you have already had, ignore that and continue.)

(b) When you have generated your five reference numbers, look up the heights of those five girls in the database.

Calculate the mean height of your sample. This 'sample mean' is your estimate of the mean height of all the girls in the database.

(c) The teacher draws a scale on the board. Each person's estimate is rounded off to the nearest cm and marked on the scale.

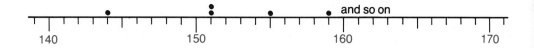

You will probably find that there is quite a lot of variation in the estimates.

(d) Now compare the estimates with the actual mean height of all the girls, which your teacher will tell you.

You may find that some people's estimates were very close to the actual value, but because there is so much variation in the estimates, you could not be very confident about an estimate based on a sample of 5.
You might be lucky and get a good estimate, but you would be quite likely to get a really bad one.

Now we will see what happens when the sample size is increased, to 20, say.

E3 Class activity

This time, each person chooses a random sample of size 20. (This can be done by extending the first sample.)

As before, generate your sample first, before you look up the heights.

Calculate the mean height of your sample of 20. This is your estimate of the population mean.

Collect all the estimates together as before.

Is there less variation than before in the estimate?

E4 Class activity

Experiment with other sample sizes.

E5 Individual work

Choose one of the following means, and estimate it by random sampling from database G.

Compare your estimate with the actual mean, which your teacher will tell you.

(a) The mean waist measurement   (b) The mean armspan

(c) The mean head circumference   (d) The mean weight

F Estimating a median

Imagine that all the girls in database G are arranged in order of weight, lightest first. The weight of the girl who appears halfway along the list (the middle girl) is called the **median** weight of the girls.

We can estimate the median weight by taking a random sample. It is convenient to have an odd number of girls in the sample, for example 21 girls.

F1 Class activity

Each person chooses a random sample of 21 girls.

Look up the weights of the girls in your sample. Arrange the weights in order, lightest first. Find the median weight of your sample. This is your estimate of the population median.

Collect the class's estimates together as before. Compare them with the actual population median.

F2   **Individual work**

Choose one of the following medians and estimate it by random sampling from database G.

Compare your estimate with the actual median.

(a) The median height   (b) The median armspan

(c) The median waist measurement   (d) The median head circumference

G   Estimating a percentage

G1   **Question for discussion**

What size of sample do you think will give a reasonably reliable estimate of the percentage of the boys in database B who wear glasses?

For the next activities you need database B and the random number table.

Note: You cannot 're-use' a random sample of the **girls'** reference numbers as your sample of **boys**, because the total number of boys in database B is different from the total number of girls in database G. If the girls' numbers were simply re-used, then the boys with reference numbers 195 to 208 would have no chance of being in the sample, so the sample would not be a truly random one.

G2   **Class activity**

Each person chooses a random sample of 5 boys, and finds out how many of those 5 boys wear glasses.
Write down the percentage of your sample who wear glasses.

If we choose a sample of size 5, the number of boys in the sample who wear glasses can only be 0, 1, 2, 3, 4, or 5. So the estimate of the percentage wearing glasses can only be 0%, 20%, 40%, 60%, 80% or 100%. So samples of size 5 are not very useful for estimating percentates.

We will now see what results we get from a larger sample, say 20 again.

G3   **Class activity**

Repeat G2 with samples of size 20. Collect together the class's estimates, and look at their distribution.
Compare them with the actual percentage, which your teacher knows.

G4   **Individual work**

Choose one of the 'yes-or-no' columns in database B, and estimate the percentage of 'yes' entries by sampling. Compare your estimate with the actual percentage, which your teacher knows.

H Scatter diagrams

For the activities in this section we shall use a different method of choosing the sample, based on the days of the month on which people were born.

There is no reason to suppose that people born on a particular day of the month, say the 15th, are in any way different from others. So those born on a particular day of the month are a representative sample of the population as a whole.

H1 Class activity

Is there any relation between height and shoe size among the boys in database B? We shall try to answer this question by sampling.

(a) Each person in the class is given a different set of five days of the month. (For example, 2nd, 5th, 6th, 10th, 28th.)

Note down the height and shoe size of each boy born on any of your five days of the month.

Plot each pair of values as a point on a diagram, like this. This kind of diagram is called a **scatter diagram**. (Don't try to join up the points!)

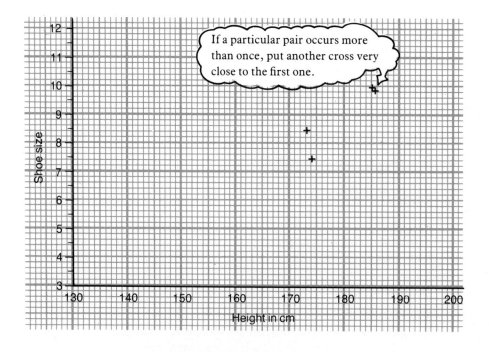

Scatter diagram of height and shoe size

(b) Does your diagram appear to show any relationship between height and shoe size?
(For example, does it appear to show that tall boys tend to have big feet and short boys small feet?)

If so, what feature of the diagram seems to show the relationship?

(c) Compare your scatter diagram with those of other people in the class.

Up to now each member of the class has generated their own sample and compared their results with others.

For the next activity, the method will be different. Only one sample will be generated, and as it grows in size a clearer and clearer picture will emerge.

H2 Class activity

Do tall girls tend to have large armspans?

(a) Each person in the class is given one day of the month. He or she looks up in database G to find the heights and armspans of all the girls born on that day of the month.

(b) Everybody draws the axes of a scatter diagram on graph paper.
Across: height, from 140 cm to 190 cm
Up: armspan, from 140 cm to 190 cm

(c) Each person then reads out the height and armspan of each of the girls in their sample. Everybody plots the points on their scatter diagrams.

Stop when you think you have enough information to answer the question: do tall girls tend to have large armspans and short girls small armspans?

H3 Individual work

Take a sample of either boys or girls from one of the databases. Draw scatter diagrams for some of the following, and comment on them.

(a) Shoe size, height   (b) Shoe size, armspan

(c) Shoe size, weight   (d) Shoe size, handspan

(e) Height, armspan   (f) Height, waist

(g) Weight, armspan   (h) Weight, handspan

(i) Waist, weight

15 Functions

A Mappings and functions

This diagram shows some points and their images after the mapping 'reflect in the line $x = 4$'.

A mapping can be thought of as a 'machine' with inputs and outputs. The inputs are points and the outputs are their images.

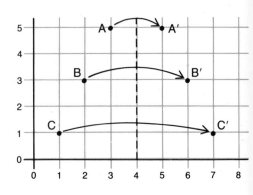

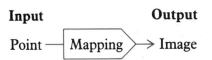

Input   **Output**

Point —[Mapping]→ Image

The idea of a mapping can also be used where the inputs and outputs are numbers instead of points.

An **arrow diagram** with two parallel scales can be used to show a mapping of this kind. The input numbers are marked on one scale and the output numbers on the other. Each arrow goes from a number to its image.

Here is an example.

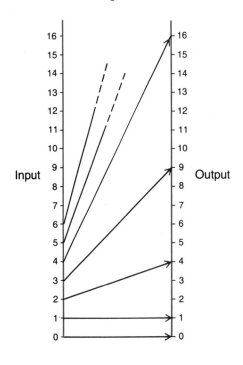

Input   Output

In this diagram, 0 is 'mapped' onto 0, which we write $0 \rightarrow 0$.

Similarly, $1 \rightarrow 1$,
$$2 \rightarrow 4,$$
$$3 \rightarrow 9, \text{ and so on.}$$

If x stands for any input, then x is mapped onto x^2.
We say that the mapping in the diagram is the mapping $x \rightarrow x^2$.

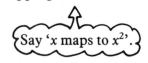

Say 'x maps to x^2'.

The letter we use does not have to be x. We could also call the mapping $u \rightarrow u^2$, or $t \rightarrow t^2$, and so on.

There should be arrows going from **every** point on the input scale. It is not possible to draw them all, so you must imagine the other arrows.

A mapping whose inputs and outputs are numbers is usually called
a **function**.

The diagram on the opposite page illustrates the function $x \rightarrow x^2$.

A1 (a) One of the arrow diagrams below illustrates the function $x \rightarrow x + 1$.
Which one is it?

(b) Write, in the form $x \rightarrow \ldots$, the function shown in each of the
other diagrams.

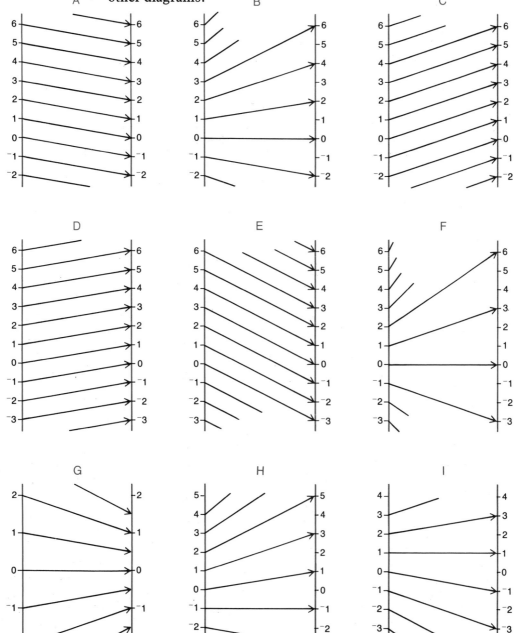

A2 Draw two parallel scales each marked from ⁻3 to 8.
Draw an arrow diagram for the function $x \rightarrow 5 - x$.

(For example, if the input is 2, the output is $5 - 2$ which is 3.)

A3 Draw two parallel scales on graph paper, each going from 0 to 12.

(a) Draw an arrow diagram for the function $x \rightarrow \frac{12}{x}$.

(b) Why is there no output when the input is 0?

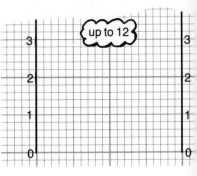

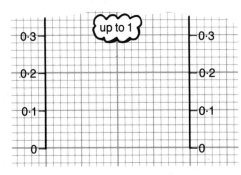

A4 Draw two parallel scales on graph paper each going from 0 to 1.

Draw an arrow diagram to illustrate the function $x \rightarrow \sqrt{x}$. Draw arrows starting from 0, 0·1, 0·2, . . . and so on up to 1.

A5 What function is shown in this arrow diagram?

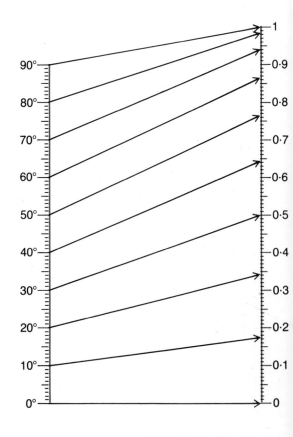

124

B Letters for functions

You can think of a function as an **instruction** telling you what to do to the input to get the output.

It is often convenient to use a letter to stand for a function. For example, we could let p stand for 'multiply by 2 and then add 3'. In symbols, p stands for the function $x \rightarrow 2x + 3$.

When we carry out the instruction on the input 7, we get 17. We write this p(7) = 17. (Say '**p of 7** equals 17'.)

Similarly, p(4) = 11, p(10) = 23, and so on.

> **B1** Let q stand for the function $x \rightarrow 4x + 1$.
> Write down the value of
>
> (a) q(3) (b) q(4) (c) q(6) (d) q(0) (e) q(⁻3)

> **B2** Let h stand for the function $x \rightarrow 3x - 4$.
> Write down the value of
>
> (a) h(5) (b) h(20) (c) h(⁻2) (d) h(⁻10) (e) h(⁻20)

> **B3** Let w stand for the function $x \rightarrow \cos x + \sin x$.
> Use a calculator to find the value of
>
> (a) w(30°) (b) w(45°) (c) w(0°) (d) w(90°)

In the example at the top of the page, we let p stand for the function $x \rightarrow 2x + 3$.

p(4) means the result of doing p to 4, which is $(2 \times 4) + 3 = 11$.
p(9) means the result of doing p to 9, which is $(2 \times 9) + 3 = 21$.
Similarly p(x) means the result of doing p to x, which is $2x + 3$.

Instead of writing 'Let p stand for the function $x \rightarrow 2x + 3$', we can write simply 'Let p(x) = 2x + 3'.

> **B4** Let s(x) = 5x − 3.
> Write down the value of
>
> (a) s(6) (b) s(11) (c) s(1) (d) s(0) (e) s(⁻3)

> **B5** Let m(x) = 4x².
> Write down the value of
>
> (a) m(3) (b) m(10) (c) m(20) (d) m(0) (e) m(⁻3)

> **B6** Let j(x) = 3√x. Write down the value of
>
> (a) j(1) (b) j(9) (c) j(25) (d) j(100) (e) j(0)

c The graph of a function

An arrow diagram is a very useful way of picturing a function 'in your mind's eye'. But it has disadvantages as a way of representing a function on paper. One disadvantage is that only a few arrows can be shown, and you have to imagine all the others. Another is that the arrows may cross over one another and make the diagram confusing.

Here for example is an arrow diagram for the function $x \rightarrow x^2$, with values of x going from $^-2$ to 2.

(Remember that the square of any negative number is positive. For example, $^-2 \times ^-2 = 4$.)

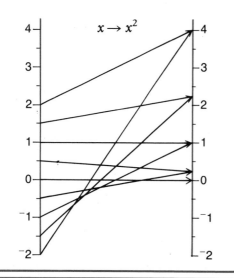

We could try putting the two number lines at right-angles, and drawing the arrows in this way.

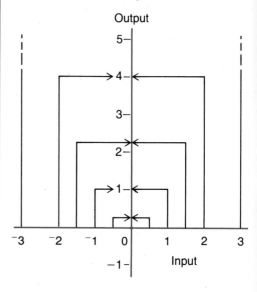

Now the diagram looks something like a graph.

A graph is usually the best way of representing a function.

Let s stand for the function $x \rightarrow x^2$.

We use the x-axis for values of the input x, and the y-axis for values of the output $s(x)$.

The graph will show the value of $s(x)$ for every value of x (within certain limits).

The dotted arrow on this graph shows that $s(^-2) = 4$.

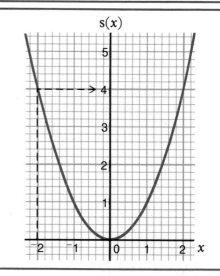

126

C1 Let t be the function $x \rightarrow 10 - x^2$.

(a) Copy and complete this table of values of $t(x)$.

x	$^-3$	$^-2$	$^-1$	0	1	2	3
$t(x)$	1						

(b) Draw the graph of the function t as a smooth curve.

C2 Let u be the function $x \rightarrow x(x-2)$
(For example, $u(5) = 5(5-2) = 5 \times 3 = 15$.)

(a) Copy and complete this table of values of $u(x)$.

x	$^-2$	$^-1$	0	1	2	3	4
$u(x)$	8						

(b) Draw the graph of the function u.

C3 Let $v(x) = \sin x + \cos x$.

(a) Make a table of values of $v(x)$ for values of x from $0°$ to $90°$ in steps of $10°$.

(b) Draw the graph of the function v.

So far all the functions we have looked at have been defined by formulas, for example $x \rightarrow x^2$, $x \rightarrow 2x + 3$, $x \rightarrow x(x-2)$. There are many functions arising in practice where there is no formula connecting input and output.

For example, think of a tree trunk.
At each height above the ground, we can measure the girth of the trunk (the distance all the way round).

Think of the height h above the ground as the input, and the girth at that height as the output. Then we have the function

$h \rightarrow$ girth at height h

We could use a letter, say g, to stand for this function. $g(h)$ means 'the girth at height h'.

The graph of the function g might look something like this.
Nobody expects there to be a formula for the girth in terms of the height.

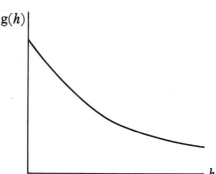

C4 This diagram shows a bottle.

$g(h)$ stands for the girth of the bottle at a height h above the base.

Draw a sketch showing the general shape of the graph of the function g.

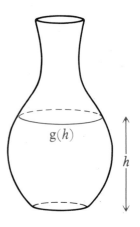

C5 Do the same as in question C4 for each of these bottles.

(a)

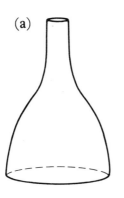

(b)

(c)

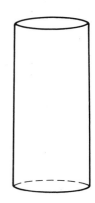

*C6 Let $c(h)$ stand for the cross-sectional area at height h.

Which of the diagrams below shows the shape of the graph of the function c for the bottle shown here?

Explain the reason for your answer.

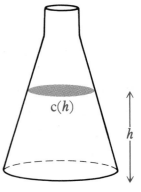

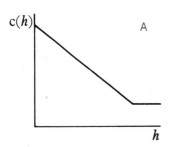

A

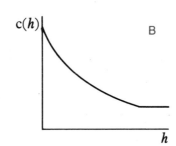

B

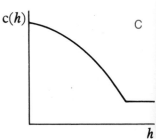

C

D The domain of a function

The **domain** of a function consists of **all the possible values of the input**.

For example, for the girth function g in questions C4 and C5, the domain consists of all heights from 0 up to the height of the bottle itself.

When we introduce a function, we should also say what its domain is to be. For example, we may be looking at the function $x \rightarrow 3x - 2$ for values of x from $^-5$ to 5 only, and we have to say this.

Usually, however, we want to allow the input to be **any** number, positive or negative (including all decimals). In that case it is not necessary to state what the domain is to be.

Sometimes the domain of a function **cannot** include all numbers. For example, it is impossible to divide by 0, so the domain of the function $x \rightarrow \dfrac{1}{x}$ cannot include 0.

D1 (a) Let $r(x) = \dfrac{12}{x - 2}$. Copy and complete this table of values of The function r. If there is no value of $r(x)$, leave a blank.

x	$^-2$	$^-1$	0	1	2	3	4	5	6
$r(x)$									

(b) Draw a graph of the function r. The graph is in two separate pieces with a gap between them.

Another example of a function whose domain cannot include all numbers is the square root function $x \rightarrow \sqrt{x}$.

A negative number, such as $^-9$, cannot have a square root. (The square root of $^-9$ cannot be $^-3$, because $^-3 \times ^-3$ is 9, and it cannot be 3 either, because 3×3 is also 9.)

So the domain of $x \rightarrow \sqrt{x}$ cannot include any negative numbers.

Every positive number has two 'square roots'. For example, the square root of 9 could be 3 or $^-3$. When we use the symbol $\sqrt{}$, we mean the **positive square root** only. So $\sqrt{9}$ is 3, but **not** $^-3$.

The graph of the function $x \rightarrow \sqrt{x}$ looks like this.

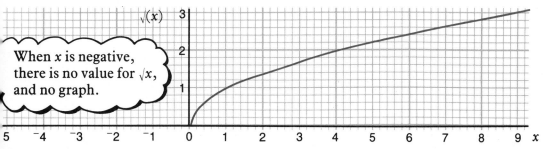

When x is negative, there is no value for $\sqrt{x}$, and no graph.

D2 (a) Copy and complete this table of values of the function s, where $s(x) = \sqrt{(x-3)}$. Round off to 2 d.p. where necessary. If there is no value of $s(x)$, leave a blank.

x	⁻2	⁻1	0	1	2	3	4	5	6	7	8
$s(x)$											

(b) Draw a graph of the function s.

D3 Let $t(x) = \sqrt{[x(x-2)]}$. For example, if x is 6, then
$$t(x) = \sqrt{[6(6-2)]}$$
$$= \sqrt{24} = 4 \cdot 90, \text{ to 2 d.p.}$$

(a) Copy and complete this table of values of $t(x)$, leaving blanks where necessary.

x	⁻3	⁻2	⁻1	0	1	2	3	4	5	6
$t(x)$										

(b) Draw a graph of the function t.

D4 Let $u(x) = \sqrt{[x(4-x)]}$.

(a) Copy and complete this table of values, leaving blanks where necessary.

x	⁻3	⁻2	⁻1	0	1	2	3	4	5	6
$u(x)$										

(b) Draw a graph of the function u.

Sequences

Let p be the function $x \rightarrow 3x + 1$.
Suppose we restrict the domain of this function to **positive whole numbers** only: $1, 2, 3, 4, 5, \ldots$

The table of values of $p(x)$ looks like this; there are no values between those shown here.

x	1	2	3	4	5	6	. . .
$p(x)$	4	7	10	13	16	19	. . .

What this table shows is in fact a **sequence**.
A sequence is a function whose domain is $1, 2, 3, 4, 5, \ldots$

When we are dealing with a sequence, we generally use n instead of x.
Also we would write p_n instead of $p(n)$.

n	1	2	3	4	5	6	. . .
p_n	4	7	10	13	16	19	. . .

E   The inverse of a function

This diagram shows the function
$x \rightarrow x + 2$.

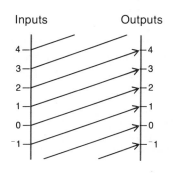

The **inverse** of this function **undoes** the effect of the function.

The outputs of the original function become the inputs of the inverse, and vice versa.

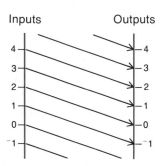

The inverse of the function $x \rightarrow x + 2$ is $x \rightarrow x - 2$.

E1 Write down the inverse of each of these functions, in the form $x \rightarrow \ldots$

(a) $x \rightarrow x + 5$ (b) $x \rightarrow x - 4$ (c) $x \rightarrow 2x$ (d) $x \rightarrow 5x$

(e) $x \rightarrow \frac{x}{3}$ (f) $x \rightarrow \frac{1}{4}x$ (g) $x \rightarrow x^2$ (h) $x \rightarrow \frac{1}{x}$

E2 (a) Draw two parallel scales, one for inputs and one for outputs, each marked from 0 to 6.
Draw arrows to illustrate the function $x \rightarrow 6 - x$.

(b) Draw the input–output diagram for the inverse function.
What is the inverse of the function $x \rightarrow 6 - x$?

E3 Repeat question E2 for the function $x \rightarrow \dfrac{12}{x}$.

E4 What is the inverse of each of these mappings?
(In other words, which mapping undoes the effect of each one?)

(a) Rotation 90° clockwise about $(0, 0)$

(b) Translation with vector $\begin{bmatrix} 3 \\ -2 \end{bmatrix}$

(c) Reflection in the y-axis

(d) Reflection in the line $y = x$

Inverse trigonometrical functions

We have met examples of inverse functions in trigonometry.
If you know an angle, say 50°, and you want to find its sine, you just use a calculator to find sin 50°.
But sometimes you know what the sine of an angle is and you want to find the angle itself. For example, suppose the sine of an angle is 0·83 and you want to know the angle. This time you use the calculator to find inv sin 0·83.

This diagram shows the function
$x \rightarrow \sin x$.

The inputs are angles from 0° to 90°, and the outputs are their sines.

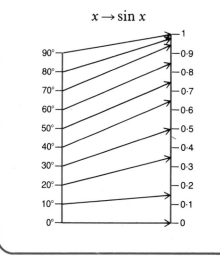

$$x \rightarrow \sin x$$

When we interchange the inputs and outputs we get the diagram for the function $x \rightarrow \text{inv sin } x$.

Now the inputs are numbers from 0 to 1 and the outputs are angles from 0° to 90°.

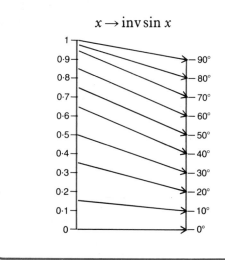

$$x \rightarrow \text{inv sin } x$$

E5 (a) Draw axes as follows: across, 0° to 90° (use 1 cm for 10°);
up, 0 to 1 (use 1 cm for 0·1).

Use a calculator to find the values of sin 0°, sin 10°, sin 20°, and so on. Plot a graph of the function $x \rightarrow \sin x$.

(b) Draw a second set of axes as follows: across, 0 to 1;
up, 0° to 90°.
Plot a graph of the function $x \rightarrow \text{inv sin } x$. You do not need to use the calculator again; you can get your points from the first graph.

16 Three dimensions

A Right-angled triangles: a check-up

A1 Calculate the side marked with a letter in each of these right-angled triangles. Give each answer to 1 d.p.

(a)
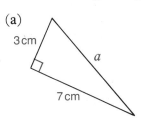
3 cm

7 cm

a

(b)
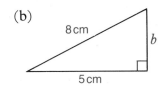
8 cm

5 cm

b

(c)
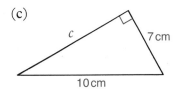
c

7 cm

10 cm

A2 Calculate, to 1 d.p., the sides marked with letters.

(a)
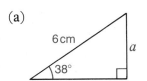
6 cm

38°

a

(b)
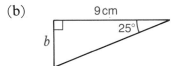
9 cm

25°

b

(c)
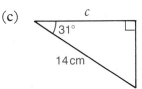
c

31°

14 cm

(d)
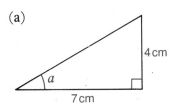
5 cm

69°

d

(e)
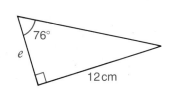
76°

e

12 cm

(f)
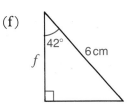
42°

6 cm

f

A3 Calculate, to the nearest degree, the angles marked with letters.

(a)

4 cm

a

7 cm

(b)
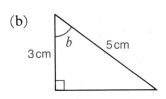
b

3 cm

5 cm

(c)

10 cm

c

13 cm

(d)

11 cm

d

18 cm

(e)

e

5 cm

6 cm

(f)
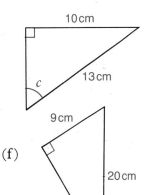
9 cm

20 cm

f

B Right-angles in three dimensions

The phrase 'perpendicular to' means 'at right-angles to'.

In the diagram on the right, line *a* is perpendicular to line *b*.

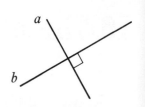

A vertical line and a horizontal plane give the clearest example of **a line perpendicular to a plane**.

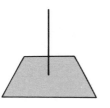

When a line is perpendicular to a plane, it is at right-angles to **every** line which lies in the plane.

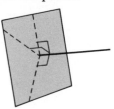

In this cuboid, the edge AE is perpendicular to the plane ABCD.

AE is at right-angles to every line in the plane ABCD, including, for example, AC.

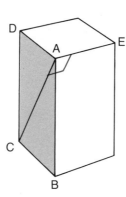

If you are unsure about this, imagine the cuboid is moved so that ABCD is horizontal.

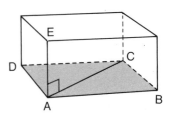

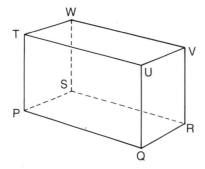

B1 This drawing shows a cuboid. Say whether each of these angles is a right-angle or not.

(a) The angle between SW and SQ
(b) The angle between ST and SU
(c) The angle between UT and UR
(d) The angle between QS and QV
(e) The angle between VW and VQ
(f) The angle between VU and VS

B2 With the same diagram as in question B1, say whether each of these triangles is right-angled or not. If it is right-angled, say which angle is the right-angle.

(a) SUR   (b) PUR   (c) TVS   (d) SPU   (e) VQW   (f) RTQ

To calculate the length of a line in three dimensions, you often have to find a right-angled triangle which has the line as one side.

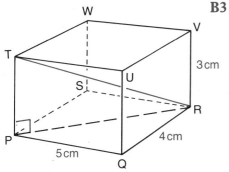

B3 The diagram on the left shows a cuboid. Follow the method below to find the length of TR.

(a) TR is the hypotenuse of the right-angled triangle TPR.
We know that TP = 3 cm, but what about PR? Calculate the length of PR. (It is the hypotenuse of another right-angled triangle.)

(b) Use triangle TPR to calculate TR.

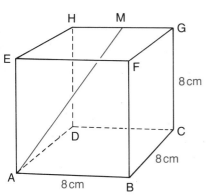

B4 ABCDEFGH is a cube; each edge is 8 cm. M is the midpoint of HG.

Copy the diagram. Join EM.

(a) Which angle of triangle AEM is a right-angle? Explain how you know it is a right-angle.

(b) Use another right-angled triangle to calculate EM.

(c) Calculate AM.

B5 The drawing on the right shows an inn sign. AB and AC are straight wires.

Calculate the length of each wire. Explain your method.

B6 The diagram below shows a cube ABCDEFGH, of edge 12 cm.

P is $\frac{1}{3}$ of the way along EH.

Q is $\frac{2}{3}$ of the way along BC.

Calculate PQ.

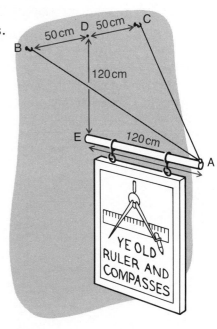

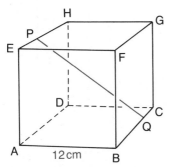

c The angle between two lines in three dimensions

If you want to calculate the angle between two lines in three dimensions, you usually have to find a right-angled triangle which contains the angle you want.

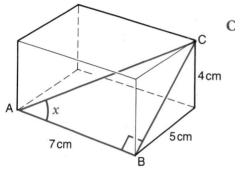

C1 In the cuboid shown here, the angle x between AB and AC is contained in the right-angled triangle ABC.

(a) Calculate BC.

(b) Calculate the angle x.

C2 Draw this diagram of a cuboid.

Add to your diagram the lines HC and HB.

(a) Which of the angles of triangle HBC is a right-angle?

(b) In the triangle HBC, BC is known to be 5 cm long.
Calculate the length of one other side of triangle HBC.

(c) Calculate the angle between HB and HC.

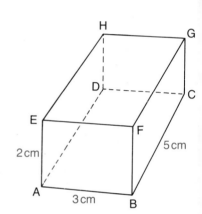

C3 Calculate the angles marked with letters. Show how you did each one.

(a)

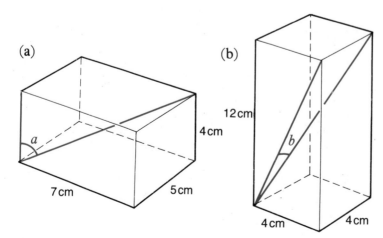

(b)

(c)

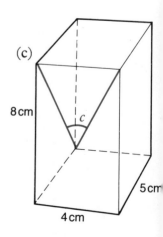

D The angle between a line and a plane

This drawing shows a wooden post supporting the side of an old house.

The post makes an angle with the ground, but different people see the different angles.

From where Aran is standing the post looks like this.

Bob sees it like this.

Cathy sees it like this.

When we talk about 'the angle between the post and the ground' we mean the angle which Cathy sees.

We can make the idea more precise, like this.

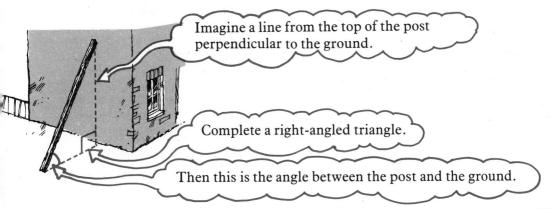

Imagine a line from the top of the post perpendicular to the ground.

Complete a right-angled triangle.

Then this is the angle between the post and the ground.

D1 This diagram shows a cube standing on a horizontal base.

AG is a diagonal of the cube.

Draw the diagram and mark on it the angle between the diagonal and the horizontal base. You will need to add a further line to the diagram.

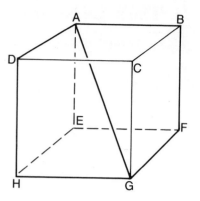

D2 Suppose the cube in question D1 has edges each 10 cm long.

Calculate the angle between the diagonal AG and the horizontal base.

D3 Calculate the angle which the diagonal TR of this cuboid makes with the horizontal base.

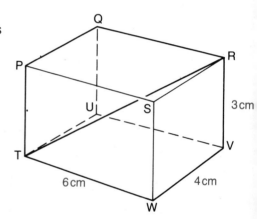

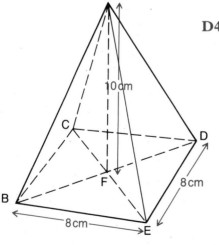

D4 This diagram shows a square-based pyramid. Each edge of the base is 8 cm long. The height of the pyramid is 10 cm.

(a) Draw the diagram. (It is easiest to draw the base BCDE first, then BD and CE to fix the position of F. Then draw FA upwards to A. Finally join A to B, C, D, E.)

(b) Mark clearly on your diagram the angle between the edge AB and the base.

(c) Calculate this angle.

The projection of a line on a plane

In this diagram *l* is a line and *p* is a plane.	From various points along *l* we draw lines perpendicular to *p*.	The angle between the line *l* and the plane *p* is the angle between *l* and its projection.
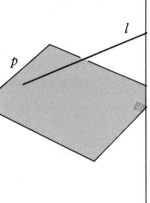	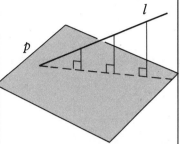 The dotted line is called the **projection** of *l* on *p*.	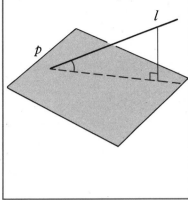

Worked example

Identify the angle between the line AG
and the plane ABCD in this cuboid.

We need to find the projection of AG
on the plane ABCD.

We know that the line GC is perpendicular
to the plane ABCD.
So the projection of AG on the plane ABCD
must be the line AC.

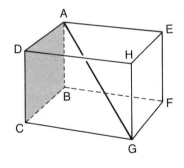

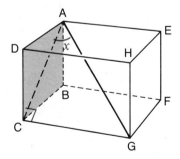

The angle we want is the angle between
AG and AC.

It is marked *x* in the diagram on the left.

D5 *You need worksheet Y4–2.*

Mark clearly the angle between the given line and the given plane
on each diagram on the worksheet.

139

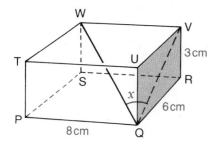

D6 The angle between the line QW and the plane QRVU is the angle between QW and QV, marked x.

(a) Calculate the length of QV.

(b) Calculate the angle x.

D7 In each case below, draw the diagram, mark the angle asked for, and then calculate the angle.

(a)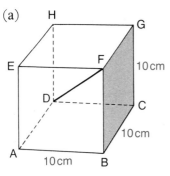

Line FD
Plane BFGC

(b)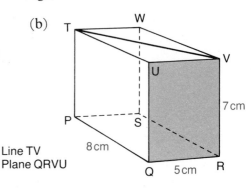

Line TV
Plane QRVU

(c)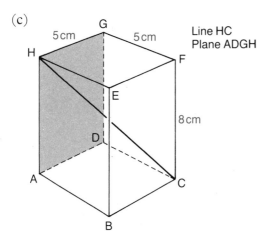

Line HC
Plane ADGH

(d)

Line VX
Plane UVZY

D8 Here again is the inn sign from question B5.

Calculate the angle which each of the wires AB and AC makes with the wall.

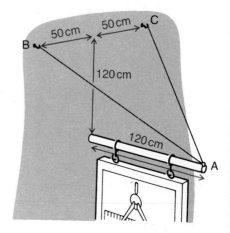

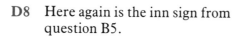

17 Quadratic functions and equations

A Quadratic functions

The path round the pond

A woman has a rectangular pond in her garden. It is 5 m by 3 m.

She wants to make a concrete path round the pond, as shown in the diagram. The width of the path is to be the same all the way round.

She wants to know what the relationship is between the width of the path and its area.

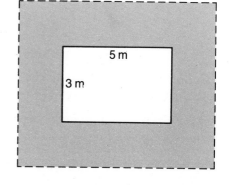

Let x metres be the width of the path. We can find the area in terms of x by splitting the path into squares and rectangles, as shown here. The total area of the path is $4x^2 + 16x$.

If $A\,\text{m}^2$ is the area of the path, then the formula for A in terms of x is
$$A = 4x^2 + 16x.$$

A graph will show us how A is related to x.

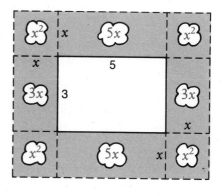

A1 (a) Calculate the values of A when x is 0, 1, 2, 3 and 4. Write the values in a table.

x	0	1	2	3	4
A					

(b) Draw axes on graph paper. Suitable scales are:
   Across: 2 cm to 1 unit   Up: 1 cm to 10 units
   Draw a graph of (x, A).

(c) Suppose the area of the path is to be $30\,\text{m}^2$.
   From your graph read off the value of x for which A is 30.

(d) For what value of x is $A = 100$?

141

The sheep pen

A farmer has 10 metres of wire fencing.
He uses it to make a rectangular sheep pen against
a wall. The wall forms one side of the pen.

He wants to know what the relationship is between
the width of the pen and its area.
(The width is marked x m in the diagram.)

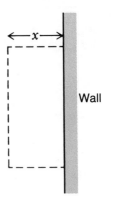

To find the area of the pen, we first need to know the length of the
other side of the rectangle, in terms of x.

There are 10 m of fencing altogether. The two pieces which are
x m long make $2x$ m. So the other side must be $(10 - 2x)$ m.

So the area is $x(10 - 2x)$ m^2.

If A m^2 is the area, the formula for A in terms of x is $A = x(10 - 2x)$.

A2 (a) Make a table of values of x and A for values of x from 0 to 5.

(b) Choose suitable scales and draw a graph of (x, A).
(You will find it useful to calculate A when x is $2 \cdot 5$.)

(c) For what value of x is A a maximum?

(d) What is the maximum value of A?

(e) For what values of x is A equal to 10?

Look again at the formulas in questions A1 and A2.

$$A = 4x^2 + 16x \qquad A = x(10 - 2x)$$

The second formula can also be written $A = 10x - 20x^2$.

The functions $x \rightarrow 4x^2 + 16x$ and $x \rightarrow 10x - 20x^2$ are examples of
quadratic functions.
A quadratic function is any function which can be written in the form

$$x \rightarrow ax^2 + bx + c$$

where a, b and c are any numbers, except that a is not allowed to be 0
(but b and c can be 0).

For example, these are quadratic functions:
$x \rightarrow x^2, \quad x \rightarrow x^2 - 2x, \quad x \rightarrow x^2 + 5, \quad x \rightarrow x^2 - 3x + 1, \quad x \rightarrow 6 - 4x - 7x^2$.

A3 Are these quadratic functions? (Write 'yes' or 'no'.)

(a) $x \rightarrow 3x^2 - 5$ (b) $x \rightarrow 2x^3 - 3x^2 + 1$ (c) $x \rightarrow 5x - 3$ (d) $x \rightarrow 5 - 3x^2$

142

B Graphs of quadratic functions

The simplest quadratic function is $x \rightarrow x^2$.
The diagram here shows the graph of this
function, for values of x from $^-3$ to 3.
The **minimum** value of the function is 0,
because x^2 cannot be negative.

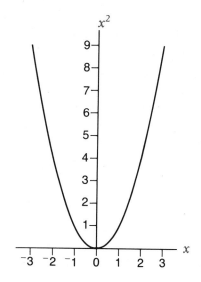

Drawing the graph of a quadratic function

Let r be the function $x \rightarrow x^2 - 3x - 4$.

Suppose we want to draw the graph of the function r for values of
x from $^-3$ to 6. The calculations for finding $r(x)$ for each value
of x can be set out in a table, like this.

x	x^2	$-$	$3x$	$-$	4	$r(x)$
$^-3$	9	$+$	9	$-$	4	14
$^-2$	4	$+$	6	$-$	4	6

and so on

B1 (a) Copy the table and complete it as far as $x = 6$.

(b) Draw axes on graph paper. Suitable scales are:
 Across: 1 cm to 1 unit   Up: 1 cm to 2 units

Plot the points from the table. The lowest point on the graph
occurs at $x = 1\cdot5$, so work out $r(1\cdot5)$ and plot this point
as well. Draw a smooth curve through the points.

(c) For what values of x is $r(x) = 10$? (Use the graph.)

(d) For what values of x is $r(x) = 4$?

B2 Let $s(x) = x^2 - x - 2$.

(a) Make a table of values of $s(x)$ for values of x from $^-2$ to 3.

(b) Draw a graph of the function s.

(c) For what values of x is $s(x) = 2$?

(d) For what values of x is $s(x) = 1$?

(e) For what values of x is $s(x) = 0$?

143

Here is the graph of the function s in question B2.

Remember that s(x) means $x^2 - x - 2$.

There are two values for x for which s(x) = 0. They are $^-1$ and 2. (They are the two values of x where the graph crosses the x-axis.)

We say that $^-1$ and 2 are the **solutions** of the equation $x^2 - x - 2 = 0$.

We can easily check that they both fit the equation.

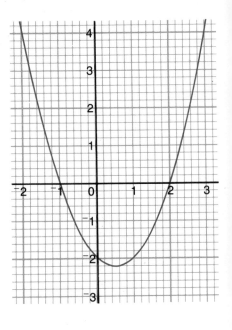

When x is $^-1$
then $x^2 - x - 2$
$= (^-1)^2 - (^-1) - 2$
$= \quad 1 + \quad 1 - 2$
$= \quad 0$

When x is 2,
then $x^2 - x - 2$
$= 2^2 - 2 - 2$
$= 4 - 2 - 2$
$= 0$

The equation $x^2 - x - 2 = 0$ is called a **quadratic equation**, because the left-hand side is a quadratic function. It has two solutions, $^-1$ and 2.

If an equation does not have 0 on the right-hand side, it can easily be re-written so that it does have 0 on the right-hand side. For example, the equation $x^2 + 5x = 2$ can be re-written as $x^2 + 5x - 2 = 0$, by subtracting 2 from both sides.

The normal way of writing a quadratic equation is to have 0 on the right-hand side.

B3 (a) Make a table of values of the function t(x) = $x^2 + x - 1$ for values of x from $^-3$ to 2.

(b) Draw the graph of t(x).

(c) From your graph, read off the two solutions of the equation $x^2 + x - 1 = 0$, as accurately as you can.

(d) Calculate the value of $x^2 + x - 1$ for each of the two values of x you found in part (c). You should get a result close to 0 in each case.

B4 (a) Make a table of values of the function u(x) = $x^2 - 2x + 2$ for values of x from $^-3$ to 3, and draw a graph.

(b) What happens if you try to find the solutions of $x^2 - 2x + 2 = 0$?

B5 (a) Make a table of values and draw a graph of the function w(x) = $x^2 - 2x + 1$, for values of x from $^-3$ to 3.

(b) What can you say about the solutions of the equation $x^2 - 2x + 1 = 0$?

144

Summary

The quadratic functions whose graphs you have drawn in this section have all been of the form $x \rightarrow x^2 + bx + c$.

The graph of $x \rightarrow x^2 + bx + c$ may meet the x-axis

at two points, . . .   one point, . . .   or not at all.

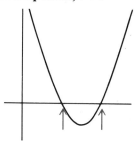 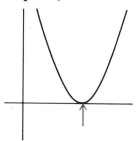 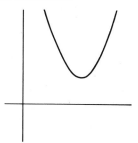

The equation $x^2 + bx + c = 0$ may have

two solutions, . . .   or **one** solution, . . .   or **no** solution.

C Quadratic functions in factorised form

The function $x \rightarrow (x+1)(x-3)$ is a quadratic function, because $(x+1)(x-3)$ can be multiplied out to give $x^2 - 2x - 3$.

$$\begin{array}{c|cc} & x & ^-3 \\ \hline x & x^2 & ^-3x \\ 1 & x & ^-3 \end{array}$$

$x^2 - 3x + x - 3$
$= x^2 - 2x - 3$

C1 Multiply out each of these expressions.

(a) $(x+5)(x+2)$ (b) $(x+1)(x-4)$ (c) $(x-2)(x-5)$

(d) $(x-3)(x+4)$ (e) $(x-4)(x-7)$ (f) $(x-2)(x+2)$

If a quadratic function is in factorised form, it is easier to leave it in that form when you are making a table of values.

Let $m(x) = (x+1)(x-3)$. The table of values of $m(x)$ can be done like this.

$$\begin{array}{c|cc|c} x & (x+1) \times (x-3) & & m(x) \\ \hline ^-3 & ^-2 \times & ^-6 & 12 \\ ^-2 & ^-1 \times & ^-5 & 5 \end{array}$$

and so on

C2 (a) Copy and complete this table as far as $x = 5$.

(b) Draw the graph of $m(x) = (x+1)(x-3)$.

145

Here is the graph of
$m(x) = (x + 1)(x - 3)$.

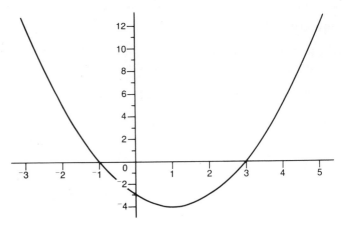

Notice that the equation $(x + 1)(x - 3) = 0$ has two solutions, $^-1$ and 3.
If you look at the table of values, you will see how they arise.

x	$(x + 1) \times (x - 3)$			$m(x)$
$^-3$	$^-2$	$\times$	$^-6$	12
$^-2$	$^-1$	$\times$	$^-5$	5
$^-1$	0	$\times$	$^-4$	0
0	1	$\times$	$^-3$	$^-3$
1	2	$\times$	$^-2$	$^-4$
2	3	$\times$	$^-1$	$^-3$
3	4	$\times$	0	0
4	5	$\times$	1	5
5	6	$\times$	2	12

When x is $^-1$, the first factor $(x + 1)$ is 0.
So $(x + 1)(x - 3)$ must be 0 as well.

When x is 3, the second factor $(x - 3)$ is 0.
So $(x + 1)(x - 3)$ must be 0 as well.

If you think about it, you can find the solutions of the equation $(x + 1)(x - 3) = 0$
without making a table of values or drawing a graph. You need to make
use of this important idea:

If you have two numbers and multiply them together, the only way
you can get the answer 0 is when one of the numbers is itself 0.

So if $(x + 1)(x - 3)$ is to be 0, then either $(x + 1)$ is 0, or $(x - 3)$ is 0.
If $(x + 1)$ is 0, then x is $^-1$; if $(x - 3)$ is 0, then x is 3.

The working is set out like this.

$$(x + 1)(x - 3) = 0$$
Either $x + 1 = 0$ or $x - 3 = 0$
So either $x = ^-1$, or $x = 3$

C3   Find the solutions of each of these equations. Set out the
working as shown above.

(a) $(x - 1)(x - 3) = 0$ (b) $(x + 2)(x - 4) = 0$ (c) $(x - 2)(x + 7) = 0$

(d) $(x + 3)(x + 6) = 0$ (e) $x(x - 5) = 0$ (f) $x(x + 6) = 0$

146

C4 Where do the graphs of these functions cross the x-axis?

(a) $x \to (x+2)(x-6)$ (b) $x \to x(x-4)$ (c) $x \to (x-3)(x-8)$

(d) $x \to x(x+9)$ (e) $x \to (x+1)(x+2)$ (f) $x \to (x-5)^2$

When a quadratic equation is in factorised form, for example $(x+2)(x-3)=0$, then it is easy to find the solutions of the equation.

When an equation is not in factorised form, for example $x^2 + 5x - 6 = 0$, we can try to re-write it in factorised form.

Factorising a quadratic expression is the reverse of multiplying out.
For example, here is how to factorise $x^2 + 5x - 6$.

1 Start with a table. You must have x here and here, to get x^2.

	x
x	x^2

2 The number in the bottom corner must be $^-6$.

	x
x	x^2
	$^-6$

3 These two numbers multiplied together give $^-6$.

	x
x	x
	$^-6$

They could be $^-6, 1$ $6, ^-1$ $^-3, 2$ $^-2, 3$

4 You want a pair which will make the other two entries in the table add up to $5x$.

	x	$^-6$
x	x^2	^-6x
1	x	$^-6$

Add up to ^-5x. ✗

	x	6
x	x^2	$6x$
$^-1$	x	$^-6$

Add up to $5x$. ✓

5 So $x^2 + 5x - 6 = (x-1)(x+6)$.

C5 Factorise each of these expressions.

(a) $x^2 + 7x + 12$ (b) $x^2 + 13x + 30$ (c) $x^2 + 9x + 18$

(d) $x^2 + 3x - 10$ (e) $x^2 - x - 12$ (f) $x^2 - 8x + 15$

C6 Factorise each of these expressions, **if you can**.

(a) $x^2 + 4x - 12$ (b) $x^2 - x - 30$ (c) $x^2 + 2x - 8$

(d) $x^2 - 9x + 14$ (e) $x^2 + 8x - 20$ (f) $x^2 - 2x - 1$

(g) $x^2 - 11x + 24$ (h) $x^2 + 4x - 21$ (i) $x^2 - 9x + 8$

You will have been unable to factorise $x^2 - 2x - 1$ (part (f) of question C6).
It does not follow that $x^2 - 2x - 1$ cannot be factorised. It **can** be
factorised, but the factors do not contain whole numbers.
To 5 decimal places, the factors are $(x - 2 \cdot 41421)$ and $(x + 0 \cdot 41421)$.

The 'table' method of factorising is only useful when the factors contain
whole numbers. If you cannot find any factors by this method, it does
not follow that the expression cannot be factorised.

Some quadratic expressions cannot be factorised, even with decimals.
$x^2 + x + 1$ is an example of this type.

Solving a quadratic equation by factorising

Worked example

Find the solutions of the equation $x^2 + 2x - 15 = 0$.

Factorise the left-hand side by the 'table'
method. The factors are $(x + 5)$ and $(x - 3)$.

$$x^2 + 2x - 15 = 0$$
$$(x + 5)(x - 3) = 0$$
So either $x + 5 = 0$ or $x - 3 = 0$
So either $x = {}^-5$ or $x = 3$
The solutions are ${}^-5$ and 3.

C7 In each of these equations, the left-hand side can be factorised
easily. Solve each equation.

(a) $x^2 + 7x + 10 = 0$ (b) $x^2 + 2x - 15 = 0$ (c) $x^2 - 4x - 21 = 0$

(d) $x^2 - 11x + 18 = 0$ (e) $x^2 - 12x - 28 = 0$ (f) $x^2 + x - 42 = 0$

(g) $x^2 - 9 = 0$ (Think of it as $x^2 - 0x - 9 = 0$)   (h) $x^2 - 36 = 0$

C8 (a) Factorise the expression $x^2 - 4x$. (**Hint.** One of the factors
is just x.)

(b) Solve the equation $x^2 - 4x = 0$.

(c) Solve these equations.

(i) $x^2 - 6x = 0$ (ii) $x^2 + 5x = 0$ (iii) $x^2 = 20x$

C9 Write each of these quadratic functions in factorised form and
say where the graph of each one crosses the x-axis.

(a) $x \rightarrow x^2 + 6x + 8$ (b) $x \rightarrow x^2 - 3x - 10$ (c) $x \rightarrow x^2 - x$

(d) $x \rightarrow x^2 - x - 56$ (e) $x \rightarrow x^2 - 4x - 5$ (f) $x \rightarrow x^2 - 16$

D Solving a quadratic equation by decimal search

If the left-hand side of a quadratic equation is easy to factorise,
we can solve the equation in that way. If not, we need another method.

The method described here is a **decimal search** method.

Let $p(x) = x^2 - 4x + 2$.
Suppose we want to find the values of x for which $p(x) = 0$.
In other words, we want to solve the equation $x^2 - 4x + 2 = 0$.

To start with, we need to know roughly
where the solutions are. We can find
this out by drawing a graph of $p(x)$.

We can see that one solution lies
between 0 and 1, and the other
lies between 3 and 4.

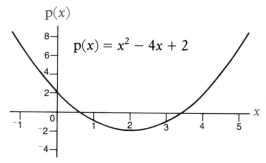

Here we will use the decimal search method to find the solution
which lies between 3 and 4. (The other solution can be found similarly.)

1 As x goes from 3 to 4, so $p(x)$ goes from negative to positive.
We make a table. We put 3 and 4 at opposite ends of the table
to show what happens between 3 and 4.

x	3	4
$p(x)$	$^-1$	2

2 Try $x = 3\cdot1$. Work out $p(3\cdot1)$.
$$p(3\cdot1) = 3\cdot1^2 - 4 \times 3\cdot1 + 2 = {}^-0\cdot79$$
$p(3\cdot1)$ is still less than 0 so we enter it at the left-hand end.

x	3	3·1	4
$p(x)$	$^-1$	$^-0\cdot79$	2

D1 Copy the table as it is so far.
Try $x = 3\cdot2$. Work out $p(3\cdot2)$.

If $p(3\cdot2)$ is less than 0, enter the value at the left-hand
end of the table.

If $p(3\cdot2)$ is greater than 0, enter it at the right-hand end
of the table.

3 So far, the table looks like this.

x	3	3·1	3·2		4
$p(x)$	$^-1$	$^-0·79$	$^-0·56$		2

$p(x)$ is not increasing very quickly, so it would be sensible to miss out 3·3 and try 3·4.

$p(3·4) = 3·4^2 - 4 \times 3·4 + 2 = {}^-0·04$
So $p(3·4)$ is still less than 0, but very close to 0.

Now try 3·5. $p(3·5) = 3·5^2 - 4 \times 3·5 + 2 = 0·25$
So $p(3·5)$ is greater than 0.

The solution is between 3·4 and 3·5.

x	3	3·1	3·2	3·4		3·5	4
$p(x)$	$^-1$	$^-0·79$	$^-0·56$	$^-0·04$		0·25	2

4 Now we work with 2 decimal places, and try values of x between 3·4 and 3·5.
It is better to make a new table, with 3·4 and 3·5 at the ends.

x	3·4		3·5
$p(x)$	$^-0·04$		0·25

> **D2** Continue the decimal search yourself between 3·4 and 3·5.
> Find an interval approximation for the solution, in the form
> 'between 3·4... and 3·4...'.
>
> **D3** The graph on the previous page shows that the other solution of $x^2 - 4x + 2 = 0$ lies between 0 and 1.
>
> Use the decimal search method to find an interval approximation for the solution. Work to 2 decimal places.
>
> **D4** Let $q(x) = x^2 - 6x + 7$.
>
> (a) Make a table of values of $q(x)$ for values of x from 0 to 5.
>
> | x | x^2 | $-$ | $6x$ | $+$ | 7 | $q(x)$ |
> |---|---|---|---|---|---|---|
> | 0 | 0 | $-$ | 0 | $+$ | 7 | 7 |
> | 1 | | | | | | |
>
> (b) Explain why there is a solution of the equation $x^2 - 6x + 7 = 0$ between 1 and 2, and another solution between 4 and 5.
>
> (c) Use the decimal search method to find an interval approximation for the smaller solution. Work to 1 d.p., then 2 d.p.

Finding a solution correct to 2 decimal places

In question D2, you should have found that one solution of the equation $x^2 - 4x + 2 = 0$ lies between $3 \cdot 41$ and $3 \cdot 42$.

If we want to give the value of the solution **correct to 2 decimal places**, we need to know whether it is closer to $3 \cdot 41$ or to $3 \cdot 42$.

Think of the graph of $p(x) = x^2 - 4x + 2$ between $x = 3 \cdot 41$ and $x = 3 \cdot 42$. We know that $p(x)$ is negative at $x = 3 \cdot 41$ and positive at $x = 3 \cdot 42$. But we do not know whether the solution itself is

closer to $3 \cdot 41$ . . .   . . . or closer to $3 \cdot 42$.

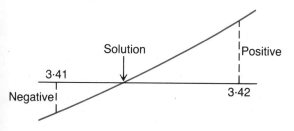 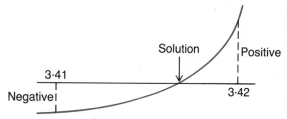

The simplest way to find out is to work out $p(x)$ when x is halfway between $3 \cdot 41$ and $3 \cdot 42$, that is **3·415**.

If $p(3 \cdot 415)$ is positive, the solution is closer to $3 \cdot 41$.

If $p(3 \cdot 415)$ is negative, the solution is closer to $3 \cdot 42$.

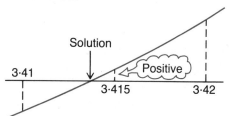 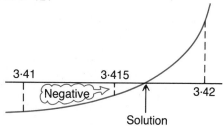

In fact, $p(3 \cdot 415) = 3 \cdot 415^2 - 4 \times 3 \cdot 415 + 2 = 0 \cdot 00225$.

So $p(3 \cdot 415)$ is **positive**. It is entered in the table like this.

x	$3 \cdot 4$	$3 \cdot 41$	The solution is between $3 \cdot 41$ and $3 \cdot 415$.	$3 \cdot 415$	$3 \cdot 42$	$3 \cdot 5$
$p(x)$	$^-0 \cdot 04$	$^-0 \cdot 0119$		$0 \cdot 00225$	$0 \cdot 0164$	$0 \cdot 25$

The solution is closer to $3 \cdot 41$ than to $3 \cdot 42$, so its value, correct to 2 decimal places, is **3·41**.

> **D5** In question D3 you should have found that the other solution of $x^2 - 4x + 2 = 0$ lies between $0 \cdot 58$ and $0 \cdot 59$.
>
> Use the method described above to find out whether the solution is closer to $0 \cdot 58$ or to $0 \cdot 59$. Give its value correct to 2 d.p.

151

D6 Let $s(x) = x^2 - 7x + 3$.

    (a) Make a table of values of $s(x)$ for whole-number values of x from 0 to 8.

    (b) One solution of the equation $x^2 - 7x + 3 = 0$ lies between 0 and 1. Between which pair of whole numbers does the other solution lie?

    (c) Use the decimal search method to find the value of the smaller solution, correct to 2 d.p.

    (d) Do the same for the larger solution.

D7 Repeat question D6 for the equation $x^2 - 6x + 4 = 0$.

E Further quadratic functions

The general form for a quadratic function is $x \rightarrow ax^2 + bx + c$.

a is called the **coefficient** of x^2 in the function; b is called the coefficient of x.

From section B onwards in this chapter, all the functions have been of the form $x \rightarrow x^2 + bx + c$. In other words, the coefficient of x^2 has been 1.

In this section we look at examples where the coefficient of x^2 is not 1.

E1 Let $f(x) = 3x^2 - 12x - 5$.

    (a) Make a table of values of $f(x)$ for x from $^-1$ to 5.

    (b) Draw a graph of the function.

    (c) Use the graph to estimate, to 1 d.p., the solutions of the equation $3x^2 - 12x - 5 = 0$.

    (d) Check that each of your estimates fits the equation, approximately.

In the next question the coefficient of x^2 is $^-2$.
You have to be careful with positive and negative when you calculate $^-2x^2$.
For example, when $x = ^-5$, then $^-2x^2 = ^-2 \times (^-5)^2 = ^-2 \times 25 = ^-50$.

E2 Let $g(x) = ^-2x^2 - 4x + 7$.

    (a) Make a table of values of $g(x)$ for x from $^-4$ to 2.

    (b) Draw a graph of the function.

    (c) What effect does the negative coefficient of x^2 appear to have had on the graph?

    (d) Estimate to 1 d.p. the solutions of the equation $^-2x^2 - 4x + 7 = 0$.

13 Optimisation

13.1 A rectangular frame is to be made from four steel bars. The two vertical bars are made from special heavy duty steel costing 8p per cm. The two horizontal bars are made from ordinary steel costing 5p per cm.

The area of the frame has to be 500 cm².

The manufacturer wants to choose the dimensions so as to minimise the total cost of the steel.

(a) Copy this table and complete it for heights of 10, 12, 14, 16, 18, 20 and 22 cm.

Height	Width	Cost of vertical bars	Cost of horizontal bars	Total cost of frame
10	50	160p	500p	660p
12				

(b) Draw a graph with height across and total cost up. Plot the points from your table and draw a smooth curve through them.

(c) Estimate the value of the height which minimises the total cost, and calculate the total cost of the steel in the cheapest frame.

13.2 A box with a lid is cut from a sheet of tinplate 20 cm by 50 cm as shown here.

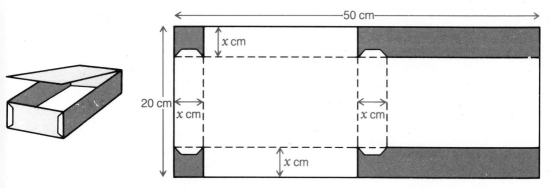

Let x cm be the depth of the box.

(a) Explain why the other dimensions are $(20 - 2x)$ cm and $(25 - x)$ cm.

(b) Let V cm³ be the volume of the box.
Write down a formula for V in terms of x.

(Continued overleaf.)

13.2 (continued)

The makers of the box want to choose the dimensions so as to maximise the volume of the box.

(c) Calculate V when x is 1, 2, 3, 4, 5, 6, 7 and 8.
It is best to set out the calculations like this:

Depth	Width	Length	Volume
x	$20 - 2x$	$25 - x$	V
1	18	24	432

(d) Draw a graph of (x, V) and use it to estimate the value of x which maximises V.

15 Functions

15.1 Let s be the function $x \to x^2 - 3x$. Calculate

(a) s(4)   (b) s(1)   (c) s(0)   (d) s($^-$2)

15.2 Let t be the function $x \to \sqrt{(x - 5)}$.
Why is it impossible to calculate t(0)?

15.3 Write down the inverse of each of these functions, in the form $x \to \ldots$

(a) $x \to x - 7$ (b) $x \to x + 9$ (c) $x \to \frac{1}{8}x$ (d) $x \to x^3$

15.4 Let $f(x) = \dfrac{4x - 1}{3}$. For what value of x is $f(x) = 7$?

16 Three dimensions

16.1 Sketch a cuboid 5 cm by 5 cm by 10 cm.
(a) Calculate the length of one of its body diagonals (the line from one corner to an opposite corner).
(b) Calculate the angle between the body diagonal and a 5 cm edge of the cuboid.

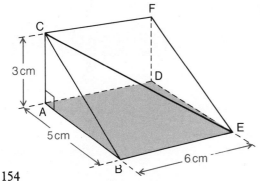

16.2 This diagram shows a prism whose cross-section is a right-angled triangle.

Calculate the angle between the line EC and the plane ABED.

16.3 This diagram shows a prism whose cross-section is an isosceles triangle (EA = EB).

M is the midpoint of AB.

Calculate the angle between the line CE and the plane ABCD.

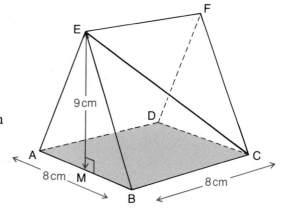

17 Quadratic functions and equations

17.1 Where does the graph of the function $x \rightarrow (x+2)(x-5)$ cross the x-axis?

17.2 (a) Factorise the expression $x^2 + 6x + 8$.

(b) Where does the graph of $x \rightarrow x^2 + 6x + 8$ cross the x-axis?

17.3 Factorise each of these expressions.

(a) $x^2 + 5x + 6$ (b) $x^2 - x - 6$ (c) $x^2 - 5x - 14$

(d) $x^2 + x - 20$ (e) $x^2 - 4$ (f) $x^2 + 8x - 20$

(g) $x^2 - 8x - 20$ (h) $x^2 - 9x + 20$ (i) $x^2 - 9$

17.4 Solve these equations.

(a) $(x-2)(x+4)=0$ (b) $x(x+6)=0$ (c) $(x+3)(x+7)=0$

(d) $x^2 - 4x - 5 = 0$ (e) $x^2 + 2x - 24 = 0$ (f) $x^2 - 8x + 12 = 0$

17.5 Where do the graphs of these functions cross the x-axis?

(a) $x \rightarrow x(x-3)$ (b) $x \rightarrow (x+2)(x+6)$ (c) $x \rightarrow x^2 + x - 6$

17.6 Let $p(x) = x^2 - 3x + 1$.

(a) Make a table of values of x and $p(x)$ for values of x from $^-2$ to 5.

(b) One solution of the equation $x^2 - 3x + 1 = 0$ lies between 0 and 1. Between which pair of whole numbers does the other solution lie?

(c) Use the decimal search method to find the value of the smaller solution, correct to 2 d.p.

(d) Do the same for the larger solution.

M Miscellaneous

M1   A mechanical toy car is fitted with a random device. Each time the car has moved 1 metre forwards, it turns through 90° either left or right each with probability $\frac{1}{2}$. Then it moves 1 metre forward again and does the same.

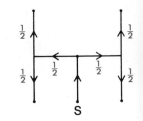

The car starts by moving 1 metre northwards from a point S.

(a) Draw a diagram showing all its possible positions after turning 3 times.
Beside each position write the probability that it gets to that position after starting from S.

(b) Draw another diagram to show all the possible positions after another turn and write the probability beside each one.

M2   Three builders have different ways of charging for plastering jobs.

Builder A charges £5 per square metre, plus a £15 basic charge to do a plastering job.

Builder B charges £5 per square metre, but makes a minimum charge of £12·50.

Builder C charges £5 per square metre, but adds a small order charge of £10 for jobs of 2 square metres or less.

Which of the graphs below shows the charging policy of each builder?

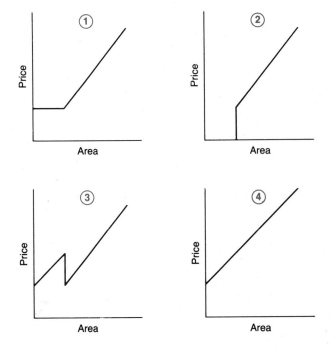

156